DISCOVER, EMBRACE, AND DEVELOP YOUR OWN DIVINE NATURE

BROOKE SNOW

CFI
An imprint of Cedar Fort, Inc.
Springville, Utah

ISBN 13: 978-1-4621-2247-9

Published by CFI, an imprint of Cedar Fort, Inc.
2373 W. 700 S., Springville, UT 84663
Distributed by Cedar Fort, Inc., www.cedarfort.com

LIBRARY OF CONGRESS CONTROL NUMBER: 2018945604

Cover design by Shawnda T. Craig

Edited by Valene Wood and Breanna Call Herbert
Typeset by Kaitlin Barwick

Printed in the United States of America

10 9 8 7 6 5 4 3 2 1

Printed on acid-free paper

To Jacob and Sarah.
May the true you shine through.

Contents

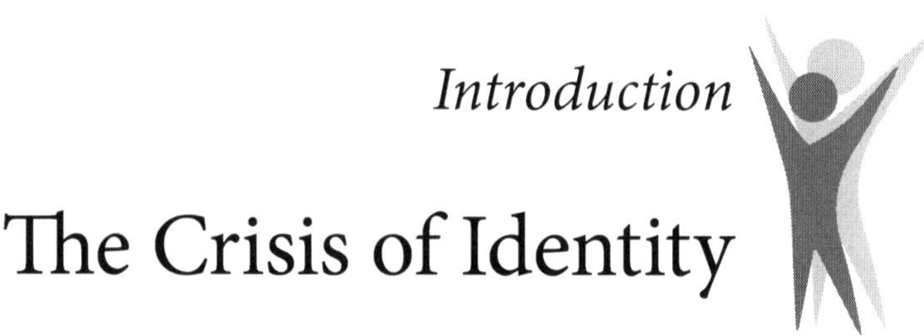

Introduction

The Crisis of Identity

You know that feeling—the feeling of comparison and not being enough? Most people feel it several times a day amidst the messaging of media. But even when the screens turn off, the thoughts in your head don't.

Perhaps you have felt those thoughts as you look in the mirror while getting ready, look at the numbers on a scale or in your personal goals, look at your calendar of commitments and expectations of those around you, or even in your relationships when you react or feel contention.

Feeling like you are not enough is an identity crisis. Most people, successful or not, feel this way sometimes. Especially when they base their worth on their performances, achievements, or approval. Identity may not be something that you consciously think about very much, yet your sense of self plays into every part of your life. Curious to see how?

Here's a quick identity check:

1. Do you ever compare yourself to those around you in real life or on social media?
2. Do you ever feel like you are not enough?
3. Do you ever feel jealous of someone else?
4. Do you ever define yourself by your faults or weaknesses?
5. Do you ever worry about what other people think of you?
6. Do you ever apologize to others for your weaknesses?
7. Do you ever judge other people or criticize them, silently or vocally?
8. Do you ever base your worth and confidence on achievement, success, or relationships?
9. Do you ever long for approval from other people in your life?
10. Do you ever feel like you don't belong?

If you answered yes to any of these questions, you have experienced the struggle of identity. We all experience this struggle! It's part of being human. We all have thoughts sparked by the questions and circumstances above, yet there is a difference between the prick of a passing thought and the weight of those thoughts turned into beliefs that shape our life.

Imagine, instead, if this were your identity check:

1. You have confidence and peace in who you are.
2. You know you are enough.
3. You easily rejoice in the accomplishments of other people.
4. You know your own gifts and continually seek to further develop them.
5. You aren't swayed by what other people think of you.
6. You can be vulnerable in life's imperfections without fear of judgment.
7. You can see the best in other people and give them the benefit of the doubt.
8. You are grounded in your unchanging worth—independent of your actions or circumstances.
9. You love and accept yourself.
10. You feel like you belong.
11. You feel abundance and are eager to create with the many resources available to you.

Living in your true identity is living an abundant life. Gone are the comparative measurements of lack and scarcity, and in their place is the vision of immeasurable worth, resources, and possibility. Living in your true identity unveils your infinite worth, your individual mission, and an array of resources to accomplish all you were sent here to do.

This is who you are designed to be. Just as the tiny acorn seed contains the blueprint to grow into a mighty oak tree, you too have within you the seed of greatness. The acorn grows when the conditions are right, and it pushes deep into the dirt to root itself for growth. When you push through the dirt of your own life with the willingness to grow, you too become grounded in your true self. You begin the beautiful process of developing into who you were created to become.

WHAT IS IDENTITY?

Webster Dictionary defines identity as, "the distinguishing character or personality of an individual."[1] It is the character of who you are, or more importantly, it is the character of who you are designed to become.

If we think of identity like a character in a three-act play, the author creates a character with unique strengths and weaknesses. He places his character in a setting and plot that will help him or her develop as he or she meets conflict and ultimately triumphs.

So too has our Heavenly Father created each of us individually as a unique character in this grand drama of life. You are here to meet conflict, develop, and triumph just as the hero or heroine of any other captivating story. Yet, unlike an actor or actress with a full script, we often wander the stage wondering who we are, what our story is, and how it will all work out in the end.

Elder Boyd K. Packer carried this analogy further when he relayed the story *The Play and the Plan*:

> The plan of redemption, with its three divisions, might be likened to a grand three-act play. Act I is entitled "Premortal Life." . . . Act II, from birth to the time of resurrection, the "Second Estate." And Act III, "Life After Death or Eternal Life."
>
> In mortality, we are like one who enters a theater just as the curtain goes up on the second act. We have missed Act I. The production has many plots and sub-plots that interweave, making it difficult to figure out who relates to whom and what relates to what, who are the heroes and who are the villains. It is further complicated because you are not just a spectator; you are a member of the cast, on stage, in the middle of it all!
>
> As part of the eternal plan, the memory of our premortal life, Act I, is covered with a veil. Since you enter mortality at the beginning of Act II with no recollection of Act I, it is little wonder that it is difficult to understand what is going on.[2]

With no memory of our life before, we have also forgotten *who* we were before. Because we each write our own ending to Act II, it becomes imperative that we become clear on our identity. The plot of our individual story rests upon our use of agency and our ability to develop into the character God created us to be from the beginning. When you know who you really are, you intentionally co-create your story with the Lord and look forward with faith to all that comes in Act III.

This book will explore the concept of identity using the following synonyms: true identity, true character, true self, and divine nature. I interpret them to all mean the same thing within the context of this book. We likewise will explore an alternate identity, which I refer to as the false identity, false self, ego, or natural man. I also use these terms synonymously.

Presenting these two identities in opposition will clearly delineate the difference between the two, helping to guide you to live the fascinating story that is only possible when living in your true character. So who are you? Sometimes the best place to start is knowing who you are not.

MY STORY: BUILDING MY IDENTITY ON SAND

I built my identity on success as far back as I can remember. When I was three years old, I began my music career. My mother had carefully watched me spend hours sitting at the piano picking out the melody of primary songs and was convinced that I was the next piano protégé. On a trip to the grocery store, she noticed a sign on the community bulletin board for music preschool. She quickly tore off the phone number and convinced the teacher to let me in, even though I wasn't old enough to meet the age requirement.

I thrived in music school. Before long, I was in piano lessons and progressing rapidly on my path to being a musician. I was playing the piano each week for sacrament meeting by the age of ten, winning awards, and gaining a lot of attention for my skill on the piano. I felt proud and important.

Piano eventually led to an interest in composing my own music, and I eagerly composed a song each year to enter into the PTA Reflections Contest, a national contest to support creativity in the arts. Every year, I would win first place in my school division. It didn't matter that there were no other entries in the music category, that blue ribbon and acknowledgement of being "first" and "the best" at something fed my ego and became an expected honor and part of my identity.

In middle school, my first-place rank now qualified me for higher-level competitions at region and state. This was where I first met Stanton Wilcox. He was a genius who also happened to play the piano and compose music. The only difference, however, was that he was so much better than I was. I stopped winning first place and started winning second place. Stanton would always take first place at the regional level and would go on to the state competition. My status had now been overshadowed. What had made me special before now made me second rate! I couldn't handle the rejection and the loss I felt receiving second place.

Unfortunately, this isn't just a story of immature elementary school jealousy. Stanton and I competed head to head all the way to college, where we both became music majors at the same university. It was like I couldn't get rid of him! Over the years, I tried to be the bigger person. I repeatedly approached him after competitions to congratulate him on his success—but in truth, my intention was to solicit a compliment in return, which never happened. I began to crave his approval and acceptance deeply. Oh, how I wanted him to tell me that I was good enough! I longed to hear him tell me that I had talent and promise.

The perfect opportunity finally came in my third year of college. One of my music compositions not only won in the state of Utah but also had placed first in the nation. I was thrilled with myself, and to the absolute delight of my prideful ego, I walked into the Music School that week to see a welcoming sign that read, "Congratulations to Brooke! Our very own national champion in music!"

The scene took my breath away! As if that single acknowledgement wasn't enough, I began to make my way to class and saw repeated signs everywhere. Every turn, every hallway, the signs continued, touting my achievement: "Brooke is a winner!" "Congratulations to Brooke!" "Brooke is a National Champion!"

I climbed the stairs to the second floor to see the signs follow me again. Classmates passing in the halls offered their congratulations. Everyone in music school would quickly know of my accomplishment, but most importantly, I imagined Stanton reading the signs. Stanton would know I was a winner, and if Stanton could see this, then I would have finally received the one recognition that meant more to me than anything else.

Serendipity continued to play into my morning as I approached the student lounge a few hours later. I'd come to study during my break, and who walked in, but Stanton Wilcox, accompanied by our professor. It was the moment I had waited for my entire life. I had evidence of my worth written on the walls, and the one person who I wanted validation from the most standing right before me, with a big obvious prompt to say what I longed for him to say.

Our professor had watched the two of us compete since we were children and instantly found this scene to be of great personal interest. He offered his congratulations and observed Stanton for a response. When Stanton said nothing, he nudged him lightly saying, "Stanton, Brooke won nationals! Isn't that amazing?"

Stanton shrugged his shoulders and walked away, undeterred. No number of signs or praise from anyone else could compensate for the rejection I felt in that moment. It wouldn't have mattered if I had just won a Grammy. I felt like a loser because Stanton Wilcox didn't validate my success.

IDENTITY CRISIS

Months later, I was called to serve a mission on the East Coast of Canada. Life was strikingly different now. Gone were the concerts, the spotlight, the stage, the recognition and admiration. My days were now spent teaching the gospel and serving in the community. No one knew anything about my past or my resume of achievements. I wasn't the "gifted musician girl." There were no distinguishing labels. In fact, I was no longer even identified by my first name. I was called "Sister," and I dressed the same as other sister missionaries dressed and did the same things sister missionaries do. I suddenly felt very ordinary with no competitions, grades, or awards to validate my worth.

This triggered my first identity crisis. For the first time in my life, I realized that I had built my entire identity on my success in music. As soon as that was not part of my life, I no longer had confidence in myself. Perhaps I could recreate my pattern of success in missionary work and find confidence again? So I practiced the only method of identity that I knew: Work hard to succeed and find confidence in my success.

I became a captivating teacher and presenter, and I worked hard to perfect my skills. I certainly developed some new talents, but if the number of converts measured a successful mission, then I was a failure. Certainly, one could argue that I still had great influence for good, but my numbers couldn't prove that. My mission ended, and I went home feeling like a nobody. At least I could return to music school and find myself again.

And so, my pattern continued. Whether it was building an identity on success in music or teaching, I was building an identity atop a foundation that could not last. An identity based on what other people thought of me and where I could find success. It was a shaky foundation that required constant validation from others and from achievements to determine my worth.

This pattern surfaced in many areas of my life. Sometimes it looked like fitting into a certain clothing size and losing weight. Sometimes it looked like having a boyfriend. Sometimes it looked like winning a competition or achieving some great success. As I got older, it started to look like being successful in my career, having a nice house, having a great marriage, having well-behaved children, having people think well of me. My confidence and worth rested upon being perfect and beautiful and happy.

The messages of the world beckon us down this path every day. Be skinny and you'll love yourself more! Be popular and you'll love yourself more! Be in a relationship with someone you admire and you'll love yourself more. Be accepted and you'll love yourself more.

One day, while listening to a podcast, the speaker shared the familiar Bible parable of the wise man and the foolish man. The foolish man builds his house on the sand and the wise man builds his house on the rock. When the rains and the floods come, the foolish man's house—built on sand—is washed away. When the rain and the floods come on the wise man's house—built on rock—it stands strong and firm and immovable.

The speaker went on to explain that whenever we build our identity on other people, achievements, results, things, or what other people think of us, we are building our identity on sand. It doesn't have any power to support us. It might work for a while—while the weather is good, but what happens when the weather changes? When the relationship doesn't work out? When our life plan doesn't work out? When people disappoint us, reject us, or hurt us? When we obtain our goals and don't feel the happiness we always thought it would bring to us? Building your identity on sand cannot last. You must build your identity on Rock.

BUILDING ON ROCK

Today, I no longer build my identity on sand. Rains and floods can come and go in my life, and my identity stands strong and true, despite the weather. Through seasons of achievement or failure, through periods of acceptance or rejection, through sunshine or storm, my identity is built on rock and doesn't wash away.

Through the use of some practical tools, which I will share with you in this book, I have learned to know, love, and develop my true self. As a result, I am confident and grounded in who I am. I feel grateful and happy almost all the time. I can look forward with faith in life, because my worth and sense of self are no longer threatened by external things.

What a relief to no longer need the approval of Stanton Wilcox! What freedom to no longer need to prove my worth or earn it. I finally know and believe deep within my soul that my worth is inherent and independen of my actions or circumstances. I can say that I truly love who I am becoming.

Experiencing life from the steady foundation of the rock is exactly how we were designed to experience life. When we live here, everything else falls into place. We make better decisions; we receive and give love to ourselves and others; we work on our personal development with hope and faith; we create great work and serve others in a magnificent way. Our challenges are manageable. Everything about life is enhanced and glorified when we know the truth of who we are and live in our true identity.

Are you ready to find the true you? The great news is that you don't have to look far. She (or he) is already inside of you. She's happy. She's always at peace. She's gifted. She's beautiful. She has a unique mission and purpose. Whether you are young or old, she's there, and she's waiting for you to let her shine.

NOTES

1. *Merriam-Webster's Collegiate Dictionary*, s.v. "identity (*n.*)," accessed April 25, 2018, http://www.merriam-webster.com/dictionary/identity.
2. Boyd K. Packer, "The Play and the Plan," May 7, 1995, Kirkland Washington Stake Center, transcript http://emp.byui.edu/huffr/The%20Play%20and%20the%20Plan%20--%20Boyd%20K.%20Packer.htm.

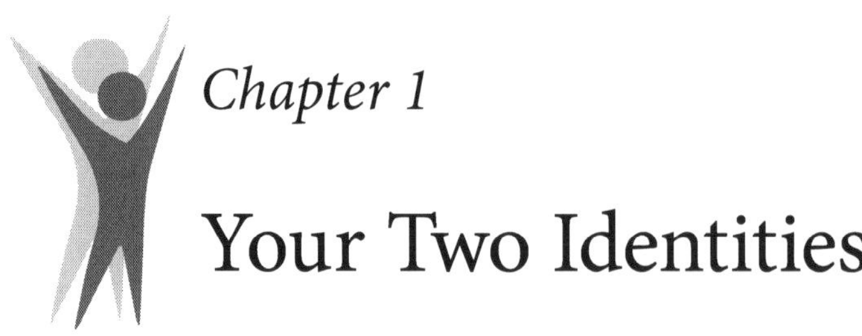

Chapter 1

Your Two Identities

Did you know you have two identities? One is true. And one is false. If you ever feel lost, feel like you don't know who you are, feel like your identity is swallowed up in your roles, feel like you must reach a certain standard to love and accept yourself, or if you ever feel less than enough, understanding your two identities will help you see what is really happening.

Every one of us confront challenges with our identities. It's part of the human experience in navigating life to learn who we are, why we're here, and how to become who we were created to become.

Identity is central to everything that happens in life. You can trace everything back to identity. Wars between nations originate from misunderstanding identity, families torn apart trace back to identity, and dreams unrealized go back to identity. When you truly understand who you are, you also understand who your neighbor is; there is respect and love for both. There is greater power to choose good over evil, to build rather than destroy, to grow rather than never realize your potential. To gain context for how this might be true, let's start at the beginning.

PURE AND PERFECT

When a baby is born, her (or his) identity is pure and perfect. We even refer to babies using these exact words. What we really see in this innocence is the baby's *divine nature*—her true self—untainted from the world's standards of acceptance. Her nature is pure and perfect.

How is this so? She embodies love. She loves herself, she loves others, and she loves the world. She finds fascination in every tiny thing. She does not criticize herself. She simply exists as she was created to exist, with love and joy.

Fast Progress

Now, if she is met with a *nurturing* environment, with loving parents who will provide for her needs, then an amazing synergy happens. True nature and nurture combine to promote rapid progress and development.

In these conditions, the baby makes astounding progress. In a short amount of time, she learns to control her physical body—to sit up, crawl, walk, and talk. Because her nature is one of love, she happily tries again. She tries to stand, falls, gets back up, stands again on wobbly legs, takes a step, falls, and does it all over again—and the nurturing environment responds with clapping and cheers.

Is it any wonder that her progress is so rapid? Is it any wonder that her development happens so smoothly? The baby's nature is pure and perfect. She loves herself. She loves those around her. She receives encouragement at every fall, and, consequently, she naturally desires to keep trying.

Progress Slows

As we grow up, somewhere along the line we are shamed. We are taught that we aren't lovable. We may be taught this by our family, our community, the media, or the adversary. We pick up false beliefs that our worth comes from things outside of us, and, unfortunately, the nurturing environment is not always there with clapping and cheers each time we fall.

When I think back on my elementary school experience, several memories surface as the beginning of my own struggle with identity: name calling or the many dreaded bus rides where I experienced ridicule. To this day, I still remember the exact moment that I saw myself from the outside world perspective. I was in second grade, and our class was walking in a line to the school library. The large halls were filled with floor-to-ceiling mirrors that reflected the light from outside. I marched along with my classmates, observing the mirrored images of each of us as we passed by. My eyes quickly found my own reflection, and I felt a shock of awareness. I was bigger than everyone else. The words *You're fat and ugly!* were shouted into my mind, and I felt immediate shame at the comparison to the other children.

More than thirty years have transpired since that moment. There have been hundreds of thousands of similar moments through the years, moments of seeing my reflection figuratively compared to those around me and feeling shame and embarrassment at what I saw. Is it any surprise that progress and growth slow down? Is it any wonder that we sometimes feel stuck, lost, and not enough?

YOUR TWO IDENTITIES

Each of us came to earth as a little baby with divine nature. God created us this way. As we grow older, we are confronted with another identity: the false identity. Psychology refers to this false identity using the word "ego." Scripture refers to the false identity using the words "natural man" or "the flesh." There is opposition in all things; therefore, you have two identities, each in opposition to the other. One is true. One is false. Your divine nature identity, or "true identity" as I will call it, never went away after birth. She's always there, only now the false identity exists in opposition.

Your False Identity

- Your false identity is the ego or natural-man self that is created through shame and the influences of this world.
- Your false identity holds you hostage.
- Any time you live your life from a place of fear, comparison, lack, contention, isolation, or not being enough, you are living in your false identity.

Your True Identity

- Your true identity is your divine nature you were born with.
- Your true identity sets you free.
- Any time you live your life from a place of love, joy, humility, gratitude, hope, spiritual connection, abundance, and faith, you are living in your true identity.

With two identities in opposition to one another, it is natural to be confused about who you really are.

I have pondered deeply upon the necessity of a false identity. Why does it exist? Does the false identity serve a purpose? Can it even be useful?

Long before we ever came to earth, Heavenly Father created the Plan of Redemption. His vision preceded the fall and the creation of the natural man identity. He intended all along for this world to be a world of opposition. For it is in the contrast and opportunity to use our agency to choose that true growth occurs. In the premortal existence, we had to choose between the Lord's plan or Satan's plan. In mortality when we choose to believe Satan we choose to live in our false identity. When we choose to believe Jesus Christ we live in our true identity. Realistically, we make this choice many times over. Yet the two identities bring different results, experiences, and eternal reward. When the Lord proves us, He is allowing us to choose who we want to become. Do we want to fill the measure of the Lord's creation or settle for a shadow version instead?

If you don't currently see your true identity, it's because your false identity is standing in the way. There is power in learning to discern between the two. We will get to know each of them in detail so you may be empowered to choose the path of your true identity and experience the joy and blessings always associated with truth.

The Two Wolves

There is a Native American legend in which an old Cherokee is teaching his grandson about life using a metaphor about two wolves:

> "A fight is going on inside me," he said to the boy.
>
> "It is a terrible fight and it is between two wolves. One is evil—he is anger, envy, sorrow, regret, greed, arrogance, self-pity, guilt, resentment, inferiority,

lies, false pride, superiority, and ego." He continued, "The other is good—he is joy, peace, love, hope, serenity, humility, kindness, benevolence, empathy, generosity, truth, compassion, and faith. The same fight is going on inside you—and inside every other person, too."

The grandson thought about it for a minute and then asked his grandfather, "Which wolf will win?"

The old Cherokee simply replied, "The one you feed."[1]

This legend is a powerful illustration of your two identities. The identity that will win—the identity that you will experience your life through—is the one you feed.

When I allow negative self-talk to play on repeat in my mind, it feeds the evil wolf. When I spend too much time on social media, my comparison mindset starts to feed the evil wolf. When I eat too much sugar and unhealthy foods, oversleep, gossip, hold a grudge, or shame my body, I feed the evil wolf.

When I practice gratitude, I feed the good wolf. When I exercise forgiveness to myself or others, show compassion, serve others, nourish my body, laugh, connect with friends and family, or pray, I feed the good wolf. Who you feed matters! The more you understand the qualities of each identity, the greater your ability to discern between the two. Let us nourish the right one.

Journal Questions

1. Do you live most of your life in your true identity or your false identity?
2. Which wolf do you feed most?
3. How do you personally feed the false identity?
4. How do you personally feed the true identity?
5. What do the scriptures say about the false identity or the natural man? (See 1 Corinthians 2:14, Mosiah 3:19, Alma 41:11, D&C 67:12, and Moses 5:13.)
6. What do the scriptures say about the true identity or divine nature? (See 2 Peter 1:4, Alma 7:23–24, Matthew 5:9, Galatians 5:22–23, Proverbs 31:10–31, Moroni 7:44–48).

UNCOVERING TRUTH

We discover who we are by letting go of who we are not. "Michelangelo is often quoted as having said that inside every block of stone or marble dwells a beautiful statue; one need only remove the excess material to reveal the work of art within."[2]

For a moment, consider the parallel to your own identity. You already have infinite worth. Your true identity is already inside you, formed as a masterpiece by

God, your creator. You can't see that masterpiece until you remove all the things in the way. At times, all you might see is a slab of marble or a statue very much in progress—until you take away everything that isn't you.

Your worth and identity are not something that you find outside of yourself. Instead, they are much like a gift. You carefully unwrap all the layers that keep it hidden and reveal a glorious treasure waiting patiently inside, whole and perfect.

This truth is such an encouragement. You don't need to be someone different to feel and know your worth. You don't need to change anything about yourself. You need only remove what's getting in the way.

WHAT IS BLOCKING YOUR TRUE IDENTITY?

The false identity and its many accessories block you from your true identity. This includes your limiting beliefs, doubts, fears, labels, and attachments. Piece by piece the false identity creates an image of who you are, drawing from both the good and the bad of your life.

Bad pieces include past mistakes, shameful focus on your weaknesses, failures, disappointments, circumstances, or unhealthy relationships. Piece by piece it constructs an image.

Good pieces can be just as illusory, building your worth out of your talents, goals, success, roles, physical appearance, righteousness, relationships, or status. On the surface, these things can be good. The struggle comes when you attach your identity and worth to them.

Seasons change, relationships evolve, goals change direction, and trials emerge. If we have built our identity on anything other than rock, these changes collapse our identity. We then lose our sense of self and try to find our bearings again.

Standing firm in your true identity allows you to navigate your life with all of its surprise twists and turns. You are steady and can see your way forward.

REMOVING THE LAYERS VISUALIZATION

Imagine all the pieces of your life that you have used to create the image of how you see yourself: Success and failure. Strengths and weaknesses. Roles and responsibilities. Imagine carrying all of these pieces upon your back. Maybe some pieces you keep hidden, and they weigh you down. Maybe some you wear with pride and want others to see.

One by one imagine taking each piece off and letting it go. Let go of the labels, the judgments, and the criticisms. Let go of failure. Let go of success. Let go of your strengths. Let go of your weakness. Let go of your thoughts and feelings. Let go of all events that have happened to you. Take each piece off and let it go.

Who you are is none of these things. They're all on the outside of you. You are not your thoughts, you are not your feelings, and you are not your past, the good or the bad.

Just as Michelangelo removed all the pieces that were not his statue, this is what you must do to find your true identity. With all these pieces gone, what is left? Your spirit, the same spirit you were born with. You are pure, perfect, and whole. You are full of light and open to all possibility.

THE TRUE YOU IS OPEN

This place deep inside you may have not been visited in a while. It is a place of complete openness because everything that was closing it off before has now been removed. We block ourselves from the light and truth of who we are by closing up.

Michael Singer, in his book *The Untethered Soul*, shares this example. He says:

> Let's say that you love somebody, and you feel very open in their presence. Because you trust them, your walls come down allowing you to feel lots of high energy. But if they do something you don't like, the next time you see them you don't feel so high. You don't feel as much love. Instead, you feel a tightness in your chest. This happens because you closed your heart. The heart is an energy center, and it can open or close. . . . When you close your heart center, energy can't flow in. When energy can't flow in, there's darkness. Depending upon how closed you are, you either feel tremendous disturbance or overwhelming lethargy. Often people fluctuate between these two states. If you then find out your loved one didn't do anything wrong, or if they apologize to your satisfaction, your heart opens again. With this opening you get filled with energy, and the love starts flowing again.
>
> How many times have you experienced these dynamics in your life? You have a wellspring of beautiful energy inside of you. When you are open you feel it; when you are closed you don't. This flow of energy comes from the depth of your being. . . .
>
> You should know about this energy because it's yours. It's your birthright, and it's unlimited. You can call upon it any time you want. . . . When you close, the energy stops flowing. When you open, all the energy rushes up inside of you.[3]

This energy within us all is so powerful that you feel it physically. Is it any wonder that the scriptures so often warn against having a hard heart? A hard heart is a closed heart. You, in effect, close yourself off to your divine potential. You become tired, tight, anxious, or depressed when you're closed.

Hard heartedness is found in refusing to forgive, distancing ourselves from God, forming contention in our relationships, refusing to change our behavior, and choosing to wallow or ruminate in negativity. We are shutting out the light and closing in on darkness.

In contrast, the scriptures speak of the necessity of having a broken heart. A broken heart is not sealed shut. It is open, even if only by a crack, the light is able to come in. An open heart brings energy, lightness, flow, peace, and joy. It is found in moments of forgiveness, hope, and the willingness to try again. It is this state of openness that connects you most wholly to who you really are. The true you is open. The more open you become, the more you connect with your true identity.

CONNECTING TO YOUR TRUE IDENTITY CAN BE EASY AND FAST

The metaphor of Michelangelo's statue is helpful for understanding the blocks that can cover your true identity. However, don't allow this image to lead you to believe connecting to your true identity will take years of hard work, pain, and suffering to chisel away all the stone blocking the way.

The truth is, you have the ability to connect with your true identity instantly and easily. What is going to take practice is staying in this space.

CONNECTING THROUGH BREATH

The fastest way to connect to your true identity is through breathing. Take a moment and try this exercise with me:

- Sit or stand with a straight back.
- Relax your body.
- Close your eyes and take three deep long inhales and exhales through the nose.
- Try it now; I'll wait!

How do you feel different right now than you did before breathing deeply? Do you physically feel more open? Do you physically feel more peaceful and more energy flowing through you than you did before? Do you feel calm? Say hello to your true self.

Just as a door opens at different degrees, so do you. The more open you become, the more light and energy you have flowing through you. Even if this moment feels like only a sliver of light, know that there is a place inside you that is always at peace and is always happy. This place is your true identity. You can connect to your true identity at any time simply through your breath and awareness.

TOOL: DEEP INTENTIONAL BREATHING

The respiratory system is the only system in the body that you can have conscious control over. Find moments to breathe consciously to connect to your true self and increase the openness and flow of light within.

Pay attention to moments you feel anxious, overwhelmed, stressed, depressed, and worried. How much are you breathing? These are closed feelings, and your breath will reflect this. If you want to instantly change the way you are feeling, then instantly change the way you are breathing so you can open up.

Notes

1. "Native American Legends: Two Wolves," First People, First People of America and Canada—Turtle Island, accessed April 25, 2018, http://www.firstpeople.us/FP-Html-Legends/TwoWolves-Cherokee.html.
2. Rosamund Stone Zander and Benjamin Zander, *The Art of Possibility* (Harvard Business School Press, 2000), 26.
3. Michael A. Singer, *The Untethered Soul: The Journey Beyond Yourself* (Oakland: New Harbinger Publications, 2007), 43–44.

Chapter 2

Hiding

FEAR OF BEING SEEN

The false identity made its grand entrance in the Garden of Eden and has been here ever since. Immediately after the forbidden fruit is eaten, "Adam and his wife hid themselves from the presence of the Lord God amongst the trees of the garden" (Genesis 3:8). For the first time, Adam and Eve view themselves from an outside perspective. They become afraid of being seen—fully seen. And they hide.

Later, God calls out to Adam saying, "Where art thou? And he said, I heard thy voice in the garden, and I was afraid, because I beheld that I was naked; and I hid myself. And he said, *Who told thee that thou wast naked?*" (Genesis 3:9–11; emphasis added).

The same deceiver who tempted Adam and Eve to transgress is the same one to point out their nakedness and urge them to hide. Satan effectively creates a false image not only of Adam and Eve but also of God.

Have you ever felt like hiding? Like it wasn't safe to be seen? We can hide physically, and most commonly, we hide spiritually and emotionally, afraid of sharing our true identity. If it's not safe to live in your true identity, a new identity must be created. Say hello to the false identity.

As you too discover the ways you may hide in your life, it is important to know who told you to hide. Where did that voice come from? Was it a voice of peace and reason, or was it a voice of panic and shame? Satan has been telling mankind to hide since the very beginning of time, and although it may not manifest in your life as plainly as it does in the story of Adam and Eve, you too experience moments of fearing that you will be exposed in some form or another.

Maybe it is fear of being exposed as a beginner, so you hide and don't share what you're working on. Maybe it is fear of being exposed as a failure, so you don't pursue an ambitious goal. Maybe it is fear of success, so you hide your gifts and talents. Maybe it is fear of wrong impressions, so you hide your successes, joys, interests, and insights, because you don't want to be misinterpreted. Maybe it is fear of rejection. It requires vulnerability to show up and be seen. What if people don't accept you or think you are good enough? Maybe it is fear of what you look like, so you dress in a way to hide or avoid being in photos.

There are so many forms of hiding. We hide ourselves physically when we don't show up and when we shame our body and appearance. We hide ourselves emotionally when we don't invest in friendships and relationships because we don't want to get hurt or to hurt other people. We hide ourselves when we don't share our gifts for fear of not being accepted or giving the wrong impression.

I have personally experienced many forms of hiding. It's no surprise to me that this tactic is one of the oldest in the history of mankind; it's one of the most unfailing and swift ways to stop your progress.

WHAT DOES HIDING LOOK LIKE?

During my years as a performer, the moment I was no longer on stage, I would hide. I falsely believed it was humble to hide. When a performance finished, I would make a beeline for the door, afraid of being seen and complimented because I didn't want to appear as someone who was prideful in my talents. So I hid.

In college, I constantly compared myself to a close friend. I felt inferior to her beauty and talent in every way. Next to her, I felt invisible and even repeated this thought in my mind incessantly: *You are invisible. Nobody can see you next to her.*

Incredibly, this mantra began to manifest in real life experiences over and over. Countless times, the two of us would walk to class and people we both knew well would say hello to my friend and stop to chat, usually never making eye contact with me to acknowledge my presence. I really had made myself invisible. I was hiding. While she enjoyed a steady dating life, I went years with only a few dates here and there. I'll never forget the day one of her eager suitors pulled me aside to say, "I feel sorry for you. The only reason a guy would ever talk to you is to get one step closer to dating your best friend."

I was hiding, and I was invisible. Not from standing in the shadow of my beautiful friend; rather, I had listened to the voice that told me to hide. I listened to the voice that told me that I wasn't good enough to be seen. I listened to the voice that told me it was humble and admirable to only take the center stage when it was my turn to perform. Shining off the stage was drawing too much attention to myself.

Physical appearance is a common target for hiding. My entire life, one of my best features has been my gorgeous, thick strawberry blonde hair. I had never believed my physical body was thin enough, but my luscious locks were my beauty super power.

A few years ago, I became convinced that cutting all my hair off would be the exact change I needed in my life. I had just had a baby and had been through a traumatic life event shortly afterward. In process of recovering, I felt tempted to reinvent myself. Celebrity pictures convinced me I could look amazing with a pixie cut, so with great courage, I told my stylist to cut it off—all the way.

In a fleeting moment, my long beautiful hair lay in soft piles on the floor, and an entire lifetime of living with long hair was now in the past. The reflection that gazed back at me in the mirror quickly revealed my mistake.

I drove home and sobbed with the impact of what I had done. Such a deed cannot be reversed. Flashes of the next two drawn-out years it would take for my hair to grow back filled my mind with horror. In grave despair, I decreed, "I must hide! No one can ever see me like this!"

At the time, my calling in church was leading the music for sacrament meeting. Panic struck me as I shamefully realized I would have to stand up in front of hundreds of people every Sunday. The thought of them all staring at my ugliness was more than I could bear. I began deliberating on how I could find a substitute for my calling for the next *year* while I waited for my hair to grow long enough to not be so embarrassing.

Most unsettling of all, I realized I wanted to hide from my own family. My parents have always loved my hair, and I feared if they saw what I had done they would be upset and disapproving. For the next year, I avoided being in any photos and never once posted a picture of myself on social media. I hid it from the virtual world, and I longed to hide it from everyone in my physical world.

As if losing my hair wasn't terrorizing enough, my body quickly put on an extra fifteen pounds on top of the baby weight still to be shed. Looking back, I see this as my body's very logical response to my desperate plea to hide myself. Layers of weight offer a form of hiding and protection. Be careful what you wish for.

Sometimes we are fully aware we are hiding, and other times we are blind. A few years ago, I closed a successful photography business to start a new business in online education. I stopped using my given name for my business and opted for *Every Branch* as my new name. I created a new brand and began publishing podcasts and online courses in personal development. For more than two years, I felt stuck in this business. I could never figure out why I felt so trapped. I loved creating, I was passionate about my topic, and yet it always felt like I couldn't breathe.

One afternoon, as I was designing an album cover for my latest podcast episode, I made a startling discovery. Staring at the screen I saw the words, "Episode 72" with a flashing cursor beckoning for more text.

The episode number and title were present, but something very important was missing. Me! My name was nowhere on the design. I was the host! At once, I began a rapid scan of every album cover I had designed in two years to see the same pattern again and again and again. Episode number and title, but no Brooke. Seventy-two album covers, four online courses, an entire website design, all representing hundreds of hours of work and two years of my life. I had not even once put my name on any of it. My face was nowhere to be seen either, as I had opted for images of nature or stock photos instead of showing my own photograph. I had inadvertently hidden my very identity in a business that was built upon me. I was a teacher and speaker, and yet I was nowhere to be seen.

Immediately, I redesigned my cover to include my name and my face. I changed my email to state the sender as Brooke Snow instead of *Every Branch* and published Episode 72. It was astounding to me what that simple change evoked. Hundreds more people opened my email than my average statistic, hundreds more listened to the podcast than my average statistic, and I began receiving private messages from listeners telling me how glad they were to see me. The only difference was my decision to stop hiding and be fully seen.

True connection comes when we are willing to be seen. When we are willing to be vulnerable. Vulnerability comes in all shapes and sizes. From sharing your feelings to actually sharing your face. We can't afford to hide ourselves. Doing so inhibits connection. It inhibits connection to our self, to God, and to others and their ability to connect back to us as well.

I know what it's like to hide physically because I was ashamed of my appearance and body. I know what it's like to hide emotionally and live with the belief of not being good enough. I know what it's like to hide spiritually because of sin and poor choices. The ways to hide are as innumerable as are the ways to shine. In every story of hiding in my life, when I have chosen to be seen, when I have chosen to open up despite those fears, I have found support and power, and I know you can too.

Is there any part of your life where you are hiding? Pinpoint any part of your life that doesn't feel good right now, perhaps a relationship, a goal, a responsibility, a certain challenge or trial, and see if you can recognize any signs of hiding. Hiding is typically justified with subtle lies. We tell ourselves it will feel better to hide. It's safer. It's quieter. It's nicer or kinder or more selfless or even more peaceful to hide. When you find how you hide, I echo the same question God asked Adam and Eve, "Who told you to hide?"

The truth is, joy is found when you step into the light instead of hiding in the dark. Faith comes when you step into the light instead of hiding in the dark. Love comes when you open up instead of close up. Every holy and joyful and energizing emotion and experience requires you to step forward out of hiding in order to receive something more. It's time to shine. The world needs the true you, because guess what choosing to shine will do?

I think Marianne Williamson said it best:

> Our deepest fear is not that we are inadequate. Our deepest fear is that we are powerful beyond measure. It is our light, not our darkness that most frightens us. We ask ourselves, Who am I to be brilliant, gorgeous, talented, fabulous? Actually, who are you *not* to be? You are a child of God. Your playing small does not serve the world. There is nothing enlightened about shrinking so that other people won't feel insecure around you. We are all meant to shine, as children do. We were born to make manifest the glory of God that is within us. It's not just in some of us; it's in everyone. And as we let our own light shine, we unconsciously give other people permission to do the same. As we are liberated from our own fear, our presence automatically liberates others.[1]

Note

1. Marianne Williamson, *A Return to Love: Reflections on the Principles of a Course in Miracles* (New York City: HarperCollins, 1992), 190–91.

Chapter 3

Getting to Know the False Self

I didn't want to go. I was overwhelmed in school from approaching midterm exams, and I was depressed. The thought of getting dressed up, scraping cold snow off my car windows, and driving on slippery roads to hear an inspirational speaker sounded repelling. And besides, it was Sunday, my only free day of the week. Why must I have another obligation?

I went anyway. My previous commitments bound me to attendance, since I was accompanying the choir that was providing the special musical number for the evening. Not showing up would certainly be noticed, and I'd be letting many people down. I dressed quickly and plowed my way to the performance hall.

Reluctantly, I joined the choir members sitting on stage as thousands of other college students poured into the auditorium. Tonight, I wasn't in the mood to talk to anyone and instead chose to keep company with my wallowing thoughts, particularly my status of being single and unattractive.

As the night wore on, I felt my emotions dipping lower and lower as I dwelled on past experiences and repeated the words in my head, *You're invisible. No one sees you.* I felt myself closing up in mournful sadness when the speaker I had been tuning out suddenly spoke clearly right to me.

"If you don't like the way you're feeling," he said, "change the way you're thinking." I nearly gasped, as if his words had knocked the air out of me, the truth ringing over and over again in my mind. *If you don't like the way you're feeling, change the way you're thinking.*

I heard nothing else he said before or after. I simply sat stunned into awareness. Never before had I so clearly seen the effects my thoughts had on my feelings. After the initial shock of his statement settled into my bones, I felt a sparkling sense of empowerment at the new idea that I could choose my thoughts myself.

Your thoughts have direct impact on your feelings. Thoughts can be broken down into two categories: what you *say* and what you *see*. Before long this triggers a domino effect: What you *say* and what you *see* creates how you *feel*. Your feelings lead to your actions. Actions bring results. Your life experience originates from the seed of your thoughts. Put into a simple pattern it looks like this:

See + Say + Feel → Actions → Results

I call this The Law of Creation. This is the pattern of everything that you create in your life. You have been using this pattern your whole life. You use it to create both positive and negative experiences.

If you are in a habit of creating negative experiences, it can all be traced back to the pattern of creation. How do you see that experience? What do you say in your mind or vocally about this experience? How do you feel? How do you react? The same can be said for positive life experiences. You can always trace it back to what you see, say, and feel.

The great news is that you can target this pattern at any moment and create something new! Choose positive thoughts, choose to see a positive outlook, and you will experience positive feelings—and what does that do? It creates positive actions and results.

If choosing your thoughts sounds difficult or laborious, fear not. I provide many easy tools later on in this book that will help you intentionally create the life experience you want to have. Understanding this process of creation is important for understanding each identity and how to consciously choose for yourself the one you wish to live in.

Satan is very interested in creation and will use this same pattern to entice us to create according to his desires. In the garden, his *words* influenced Adam and Eve to *see* their nakedness, *feel* shame, and *react* by hiding. So, the adversary will influence us in the same way to create a false identity. In what ways does the adversary seek to influence us to create a false identity?

SEEING FALSE PERCEPTIONS THROUGH . . .

- self-criticism
- criticism of others
- pride/comparison
- perfectionism
- unrealistic expectations of yourself and others
- worth tied to external validation, standards, or approval
- labels

SAYING FALSE WORDS

- You are not _____ enough.
- You can't because _____.
- You are too different.
- You don't belong.
- Life is hard. There is so much struggle.
- If you could only _____, then you would be loved and belong.
- If only _____ would happen, then you would be loved and belong.

- You are better than someone else because _____.
- You are less than someone else because _____.

These false words begin as "you" statements because they come from outside of us. In time, they evolve into "I" statements. "You are not enough" turns to "I am not enough" as we are enticed to accept these statements as the truth of who we are. If we repeat them long enough, we begin to create opposition to our divine destiny.

FEELINGS THAT FEED THE CYCLE

- anxiety
- fear
- stress
- anger
- resentment
- bitterness
- guilt
- shame
- unworthiness
- worthlessness
- disappointment
- pride
- jealousy
- being stuck
- being overlooked
- selfishness

You can always match these feelings with corresponding words and images. *If you don't like the way you're feeling, change the way you're thinking.* Use these feelings as a clue to find the words and images that are feeding the cycle.

Living in your false identity does not feel good because it is out of alignment with the truth of who you really are. If these perceptions and words were true, they wouldn't make you feel so bad.

God has promised us that we can know the truth of all things through the power of the Holy Ghost (Moroni 10:5). Further, we recognize the truth spoken by the Holy Ghost through the feelings of "love, joy, peace, longsuffering, gentleness, goodness, faith" (Galatians 5:22). When you are living in alignment with your true identity, you will feel these wonderful feelings and know you are home.

TELLING YOURSELF STORIES

If allowed to stay long enough in your thoughts, the adversary begins to influence you to create a false identity. You form a picture of how you see yourself. Not only that but also you create a false world to interact in. Similar to donning a costume, glasses, and walking into a circus fun house, you now see everything and everyone with great distortion. It is a false reality. A world that isn't true.

Brené Brown, in her book *Rising Strong* talks about this false reality, stating, "The most dangerous stories we make up are the narratives that diminish our inherent worthiness."[1] When you live in your false identity, you tell yourself stories about how other people see you, what they're thinking about you, and what happens to you, all to support this world you see and live in. It can be as small as catching an eye roll or glance from someone across the room and telling yourself a story about how he or she doesn't like you. It can be bigger things like important relationships in your life where you have repeatedly told yourself the same stories over and over to the point of creating conflict and limiting beliefs.

For example, when my son was around three years old, parenting suddenly became infinitely more difficult. I was a first-time parent and found myself with an extremely active child who I didn't know how to manage. He was always on the move, and his driven, intense nature seemed to constantly be pushing me to the edge. Going places in public became a challenge I dreaded, most especially attending church. Sitting in a pew and quietly listening to a speaker felt next to impossible for his curiosity and energy. Any sign of misconduct would set my body on alert, and I began to tell myself a story that everyone in the congregation was looking at me, disapproving of me, and deliberating on what a poor mother I was to have such an unruly child. During countless Sundays, I would leave in the middle of the meeting with my son in tow to escape to the hallway, not just to provide some peacefulness to the congregation, but more so to escape the stares and judgments of the other church members I was so convinced were criticizing me.

I'd walk the halls with this story penetrating my thoughts and look at my child to repeatedly wonder at "how difficult" he was. I thought, *He's so hard! He won't listen! What am I doing wrong? Why can't I parent better? I'm such a bad mother!*

After a few months of having this story in my head, I began to dread not only going to church but also my day-to-day life, which was filled with anxiety at my inability to function as a mother. I was convinced I had the most difficult child and that something must be wrong with him or me because we were completely unable to make it through the day without either one of us breaking down in a tantrum. By the grace of God, a mentor crossed my path that shifted my mindset. She helped me to see how the story I was telling myself was creating my experience. The way I *saw* him and the words I would *say* about him were creating my *feelings*. And my feelings were causing us both to react and create contention.

Over the next few months, I practiced *seeing* my son differently. I began to observe his innate talents, already apparent even at a young age. I began to *talk* about him differently in my mind and also to other people. With consistent practice, I began to truly believe my words, and the way I saw him changed. My feelings changed, which changed my actions. Life began to feel lighter, happier, more manageable, and even fun. My son's behavior changed because I had changed. I had chosen a different story to tell, and everyone was the better for it.

Families are torn apart all the time because of the stories that we tell ourselves. Wars are started because of the stories that we tell ourselves. There are friendships that are never made, discoveries and inventions never found, wonderful art that is never created, peace that never comes, simply because of living in the false identity.

We don't have to live in a false world. The brilliant and wonderful news is that everything changes when we live in our true identity and tell a better story. Other people change and we change. Why? Because we see differently. We start to see things as they really are. Truth is able to finally surface, and we open up.

RECOGNIZING THE FALSE IDENTITY ON EVERY LEVEL

When I walked you through the breathing exercise to connect to your true identity, we learned the true identity is a place of openness. This openness allows light and energy to flow freely through you. This openness is spoken of in scripture with words such as "broken heart."

In direct contrast, the false identity always has a degree of closure. The thoughts, perceptions, and feelings of the false identity thrive on separateness and close you off from truth and light. Scripture identifies this state of closure using words such as "hard heart" and "stiff neck."

So how can you come to recognize when you are open or closed? How do you recognize when you feel the false identity directing your experience?

Tightness in Body (Your Physical Self)

Your physical body will always tell you if you are open or closed. When the false identity tries to take over in my life, I often feel tightness in my chest, as my heart starts to close off in protection. Other times, I may feel it in my stomach, my gut closing off in fear or anxiety about something happening in my life. I can also feel it in my shoulders as tension from the false identity and when I feel alone in my burdens. My body feels heavier and my movement is not as fluid or flexible. It takes a lot more energy for me to move. My breathing is always shallow, and at times, I find I am not breathing at all.

Learn to pay attention to how your body feels when you know the false identity is dominating. Become very familiar with how that manifests in your own body. Do you feel tight? Stiff? Sore? Heavy? How is your breathing?

Your body is an amazing tool and guide for you in your life. As you learn to listen to what it is saying to you, you will have greater discernment in seeing the truth from the error in the world around you (and within you).

Just a few days ago, I sat in Sunday School listening to a wonderful discussion regarding the great role of women, and I immediately felt my chest tighten and my breathing stop. As if on cue, I started telling myself a story about how I didn't measure up to the standard of women they were talking about. My husband was sitting next to me, and I embellished that story to include how he must surely be listening to this dialogue feeling like he got the short end of the stick marrying me.

I pushed the thoughts aside, but the tight feeling in my chest stayed. Thankfully, I knew this tight feeling was a signal to me that I was closing off. I could also match the tight feeling with the story I was telling myself. They went hand in hand and fed off each other. Because I recognized this, I could discern truth from error and knew that my false identity was hungry and wanted to be fed. The great thing about breath is that I used it to help myself even in a public setting. I indiscreetly took a few moments and focused on breathing deeply in and out to help open my heart again.

Trapped Emotions (Your Emotional Self)

Your feelings are a powerful clue. When your heart is closed, the emotion you experience gets trapped in your body instead of flowing through you, often showing up in your physical body as the tightness we have just discussed. Have you ever felt the emotions of anger, anxiety, fear, shame, jealousy, resentment, or unworthiness get trapped inside your body? You know they're trapped when the feeling has not passed within a minute or two and also if they are triggered by something you see or hear that fires them up again.

Maybe you've had a good day when suddenly, you see someone from your past that you've had conflict with. Instantly the good feelings you had before are overshadowed by panic, fear, resentment, or jealousy. You may have had no interaction with this person, yet even the sight of them conjures these past feelings. The rise of these emotions signals that you have trapped emotion inside you. If you had processed these emotions when you felt them the first time, they wouldn't be triggered again merely upon sight.

To be clear, the false identity is *not* the negative emotion itself—you can still feel negative emotions in your true identity, but the false identity will trap the emotion through a closed heart. This causes you to suffer the pain and burden of carrying the negative emotion indefinitely until you choose to open up and let it go.

Limiting Beliefs (Your Mental Self)

A limiting belief is a false belief that you acquire when you make an incorrect conclusion about something in life. For example, a person could acquire a limiting belief about his or her ability to succeed stemming from an experience of failure. "I can't do it. I am a failure. I don't have the ability." Over time, these beliefs are collected and influence your life in negative ways. Most importantly, they force you to live below your potential. You can gather these beliefs from your own mindset or from the words other people say to you in your life.

When I completed my first year of voice lessons from a highly accredited teacher, her final analysis of my progress left me with a limiting belief I carried for many years. "Brooke, you have come a long way this year," she said. "I think one thing we can work on going forward is creating a more beautiful sound!"

No matter how she worded it, all I heard was the loud interpretation from my false identity, "You have a horrible sounding voice. Give up. You weren't born to be a singer." This limiting belief ended my voice training. I never took another lesson, convinced I wasn't gifted enough.

Unfortunately, I didn't understand that most talents are not innate but rather developed. To make such a final analysis as a beginner is foolish. Life is all about developing. When we carry limiting beliefs, we block ourselves from growth and opportunity.

The false identity whispers limiting beliefs to your mind and reinterprets or ruminates upon the words others may say to you. Through this repetitive storytelling, you take upon these beliefs as part of who you think you are. Limiting beliefs keep you from trying new things, from developing your gifts, from cultivating friendships, from overcoming trials and obstacles, and ultimately, from growth. It is a closed mindset, limiting you in progress.

Limiting beliefs are often characterized by their sweeping generalities and black and white nature. You can't _____. You never _____. You always _____. You are _____. We likewise form limiting beliefs about others: He can't _____. She never _____. He always _____.

If you find yourself stuck or blocked in any area of your life, ask yourself, "What do I believe that is causing me to feel this way?" Learn to question your beliefs, get curious about them, explore whether they are open or closed in nature, and choose whether they are worth keeping. If not, choose a true belief that frees you to progress again.

Darkness (Your Spiritual Self)

While trapped emotions block your emotional self, and limiting beliefs block your mental self, it is darkness that blocks your spiritual self. By now, you likely see the contrast between the false identity and the true identity, symbolized in the very qualities of light or dark.

Your true identity is a place of pure light, whereas the false identity is a shadow. This is brilliantly depicted in nature by the moon's rotation around the earth. When the side of the moon we see from earth is fully facing the sun, it completely reflects the light of the sun. We call this a full moon. When the side of the moon we see from earth is completely turned away from the sun, it is in complete shadow. We call this a new moon. In its full orbit around the earth, the moon will wax, increase in light, and wane, decrease in light, completely dependent upon one factor: its orientation to the sun.

I am continually fascinated by the parable of the moon's light. When I am fully facing toward the Son of God, I shine! I am filled with light. I am open and receiving. When I am turned away from the Son of God, I am in shadow. I do not shine. I am dark.

Most of us experience life somewhere in between a full moon and new moon. I like to ask myself whether I am waxing or waning. Am I increasing in light or decreasing? Am I opening or closing? When the false identity is allowed to stay for a visit, we will wane in light. We can learn much about darkness by studying its opposite.

In Doctrine and Covenants 84:45, we learn: "For the word of the Lord is truth, and whatsoever is truth is light, and whatsoever is light is Spirit, even the Spirit of Jesus Christ." Here, light and truth are synonymous. Is it any wonder the false beliefs blocking your mental self originate from darkness? Light is truth and darkness is false.

Verse 46 gives additional insight: "And the Spirit giveth light to every man that cometh into the world; and the Spirit enlighteneth every man through the world, that hearkeneth to the voice of the Spirit." Every man and woman in the world has been endowed with this light! And this light is enlightened when we hearken to the voice of the Spirit—when we face the Son.

There is no question about whether you are a being of light. If you don't feel the light within you, then you simply need to turn around. Remember who you are. You are not your emotions, you are not your limiting beliefs, and you are not darkness. The true you is light and truth. The true you will shine when you face toward the Son.

Journal Questions

1. What stories do you suspect you have been telling yourself? Stories about you, other people, and circumstances in your life?
2. In what ways do you feel the false identity in your body?
3. How have you experienced trapped emotions?
4. What are some of your prominent limiting beliefs? Are you ready to change them?
5. Have you felt the difference between spiritual light and darkness? In what ways?

Note

1. Brené Brown, *Rising Strong* (New York: Spiegel & Grau, 2015), 76.

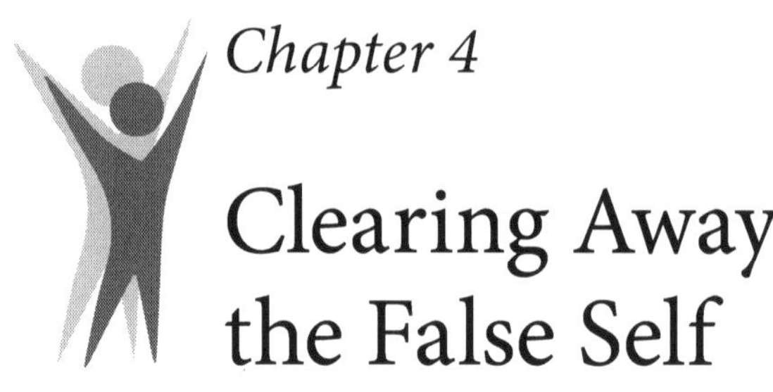

Chapter 4

Clearing Away the False Self

"If you don't like the way you're feeling, change the way you're thinking." These words still ring in my ears today. Twenty years have passed since that long-ago winter evening when my ruminating thoughts were finally convicted for causing depression. After this discovery, I carried a fascination that my thoughts had power to create my feelings. Unfortunately, beyond the inspirational message these words embody, I lacked the knowledge of how to make it practical. How do I change something so ingrained from incessant practice?

It's one thing to simply pick a new thought in the moment, which is helpful, but what about all the times I am not even aware of my thoughts? Can I catch them in the act before they do damage? Can I program my mind to think something different? Can I really change how I feel? Turns out you can.

CLEARING TOOLS

Today, my toolbox for clearing the false identity is packed full, and I eagerly add more tools when I find them. These tools are practical, and most importantly, they work. Use them whenever your false identity emerges. Some tools are fast acting, while others require a bit more time and focus to work on a deeper level. The beauty of having many to choose from lies in your ability to customize your prescription for what you need in the moment.

Clearing tools remove the layers on top of your true self. These layers include the labels, limiting beliefs, negative emotions, doubts, fears, resentments, and attachments that cover up who you really are. Each layer removed brings your true identity closer to the surface.

After mentoring a student of mine for a few weeks, I loved how she described the new way she was feeling: "I feel a spark inside myself. I feel my true self being found once again." Your true self is more than a spark, your true self is full of light and truth. It's time to clear away the layers that stand in the way so she can fully shine. Here are eleven of my favorite tools to accomplish this:

CHANGING WHAT YOU SAY

CLEARING TOOL #1: THE LITTLE BLACK NOTEBOOK

How do you clear the negative words out of your mind? Write them down.

Sometimes thoughts will call out to you again and again until you turn and face them. When you give your thoughts life on paper instead of life in your head, they will leave you. You want them outside of you, not inside.

This clearing tool is simple and fast. Obtain a simple black throwaway notebook. The spiral-bound, ninety-nine-cent version found at the grocery store is a great option. Use the blank pages to jot down any negative thoughts that call out to you. It's a black journal for your dark thoughts. Hold nothing back and dictate the words exactly as they sound in your mind, ugly, awful, and degrading as they may be. When you're done, rip the page out and shred it, crumple it up, and throw it away. I choose this tool when my thoughts are targeting my identity. The words that appear on the page often take a second person point of view. You are _____. You can't _____.

The difference between first-person "I" statements and second-person "you" statements is important to note. All negative thoughts originate first from the adversary. It is upon repetition that we adopt these as our own beliefs and later change the statement to first person. When I can literally see "you" statements on the page before me, it is a powerful reminder that this is not who I am. Though I may hear these words in the voice of my mind, they are coming from Satan as an enticement to live in opposition to my true identity.

You will experience an emotional release simply from getting the words out of your head. Don't be surprised when the words really do leave your mind. You gave them life on paper and not in your head.

CLEARING TOOL #2: WRITE AND BURN

This clearing tool is deep and intense. When your negative feelings stem from a situation, relationship, or limiting belief, consider the write and burn tool. This takes a bit more time to complete but is worth the added focus and allows all the associated emotion and limiting beliefs to surface and ultimately be cleared from your body on every level.

GUIDELINES

1. Allow yourself a good amount of time, about fifteen to thirty minutes.
2. Decide to complete this exercise in one sitting. Do not let this remain unfinished. You may have deeply rooted emotions and thoughts arise that feel so potent you think that surely you'll be stuck writing forever. This is a false belief. Decide to complete this clearing tool in one sitting, and you will.

3. Pray first. Ask God to release the limiting beliefs and emotions from you on every level: physically, mentally, emotionally, and spiritually.
4. Begin with the prompt: "When I think about _____, I feel _____."
5. Write out all thoughts and feelings that come up, word for word with no censorship.
6. At some point, you will feel a shift from darkness to light. Your words will change and your feelings will change. You'll know when you're done writing.
7. Pray another prayer of gratitude.
8. Burn or discard your writing. It's done and gone forever.

CHANGING WHAT YOU SEE

Clearing Tool #3: Look Somewhere New

"Come into my office, sisters," my mission president urged with kindness. We had stopped by to pick up our mail, but at a glance the emotional burdens we were carrying were apparent in our demeanor. He could see our heavy shoulders and fallen countenances. We were struggling as a companionship to stay positive and have faith in our own ability as missionaries. We eagerly followed his gesture towards his open door leading to his private office and sat down in relief. We ached for counsel. How can we find our way out of being stuck?

He listened briefly to our story of struggle before quickly identifying the root of our problem: our thoughts and, in particular, the way we see.

"I'm not a good teacher," my companion complained. "I can't remember everything I'm supposed to say," she muttered near tears.

"The people we teach aren't ready to make changes in their lives," I added later, piling up the evidence of all the things going wrong in our life. Whether it was the way we saw ourselves or the people around us, we had very clear images of limitation. I can't. We can't. They won't. We described everything in drab detail and waited for his lightning bolt of revelation that would zap our lives back to full color.

"What do you do when a bad thought comes to you?" he asked me. I stumbled, surprised by his question. What did this have to do with our problems? Did he think I had impure thoughts?

"Um, sing a hymn?" I offered up as a common suggestion I had heard through my childhood.

He smiled. "That is a good and useful tool," he admitted. "Let me tell you what I do."

I sat up in alert attention. More than the counsel that awaited, I was intrigued that this spiritual giant of a man had just admitted to having bad thoughts. I had secretly hoped that once a person had reached his or her level of spiritual maturity that such snares wouldn't reach up to him or her. My disappointment at the idea of living the rest of my life with the forces of opposition always at hand faded into a sense of relief that he was just like me. Human. There was hope for me yet.

"When a bad thought comes to me," he stated, "I look somewhere new." He saw our confused faces and expounded in detail. "I change my focus. Literally. I look at the window. Or I look at the picture on the wall. Or I look at the door handle or the tree across the street," he said matter-of-factly. "Your mind can't continue to hold the thought or image when you change your focus. Just watch. If you dwell on a thought, your eye is still and likely unfocused. But change your focus and look somewhere new, and the thought vanishes. If it comes back, repeat the process."

I practiced this new tool with great curiosity. With a laugh of amazement, I realized that it worked! Sometimes I'd end up refocusing around the room in several different places, but always, with each refocus, my mind instantly cleared until I allowed a new thought to enter.

Use this tool to redirect unwanted thoughts as they enter your mind. It's fast and especially useful in moments you are in public or unable to spend time writing anything down.

Clearing Tool #4: Get Grounded in Nature (Mother Nature's Remedy)

Have you ever felt the transformation of being in a state of stress, anxiety, anger, or sadness and have it all completely melt away when you spend time in nature? Ruminating on thoughts and feelings brings imbalance to your body because you are living too much inside your head. Going for a walk or run outside, laying in the grass, sitting next to a stream, hiking through a forest, or even visiting a city park will quickly rebalance the way you feel. You connect your body back to the earth. This grounding effect is powerful and necessary to your own spiritual, mental, emotional, and physical health.

Those who live in extreme weather conditions of blistering hot summers, weeks of rain and cloud cover, or frigid cold winters, know the challenge of finding time to be in nature when nature seems quite uninviting. After listening to a study performed on the cognitive benefits of nature, I laughed out loud.

The first study compared the cognitive performance of a group of people asked to spend thirty minutes outdoors every day to a control group who did not. As expected, the nature group scored much higher. But just to be sure that it really was the effect of nature, and not just the happy feelings that come from being outside in a pleasant environment that influenced the results, the researchers conducted the same study in the dead of winter in Northern Maine and asked participants to spend thirty minutes outside every day in the freezing cold. They too outperformed the control group who did not spend time outside.[1] Turns out nature still grounds us, even if conditions aren't perfect.

It just so happened that I heard this study in mid-winter, where my hometown regularly dips below freezing temperatures for weeks or even months at a time. I usually avoid time outside from December to February and wait till it's pleasant enough to experience those happy feelings that were suspect in swaying the study.

Curiosity led me, days later, to bundle up in my long red down-feather coat with my triple-layer clothing strategy of warmth to head outside in the dark of night. I simply walked the streets of my neighborhood for forty-five minutes, my eyes and nose the only part of me exposed to the icy night air. My brisk walk helped keep my body temperature high enough to make the excursion bearable, and, before long, I found out that happy feelings can be experienced even when the earth is frozen. I returned home feeling like a new woman and vowed to spend more time outside, even when the rest of the world around me is hunkering safely inside. I may not go out every day during the winter, but I learned very quickly that it's still an option for those days I really need the extra help of getting out of my head.

Regardless if the weather is dreamy or forbidding, I always return home feeling more myself. The real me. The true me. I'm no longer stuck in my head but reconnected to the earth that is made of the same matter as my body and created by the same hand.

In the words of God Himself, "Yea, all things which come of the earth, in the season thereof, are made for the benefit and the use of man, both to please the eye and to gladden the heart; Yea, for food and for raiment, for taste and for smell, to strengthen the body and to enliven the soul" (D&C 59:18–19).

Clearing Tool #5: Become the Observer

Viktor Frankl states, "Between stimulus and response there is a space. In that space is our power to choose our response. In our response lies our growth and our freedom."[2]

The first step to changing your life is awareness. When you find yourself closing up or separating yourself, become the observer. Becoming the observer is all about the art of noticing. Notice what your body is doing. Notice what your mind is thinking. Notice how you are seeing and simply observe it as if it were all flowing past you.

For example, when I am feeling stress and annoyance from the high-energy demands of my children, I can lose my temper and easily get frustrated if I am not conscious of my actions. If I were experiencing these feelings and chose to become the observer in these moments, I would think to myself, *Wow, Brooke. You are feeling upset. Do you see how your chest is tight and your fists are clenched? Do you notice that you are actually holding your breath right now? It's so interesting!*

Or what if I am scrolling through social media, and I find myself triggered by a friend's post. I start to feel jealousy and compare myself to her, believing I am less than enough. If I become the observer in this moment, then I will think *Brooke, it's so interesting that you're getting triggered right now. Look at that! You feel jealous. How does the jealousy feel? Feel it.*

Michael Singer in his book *The Untethered Soul* describes it this way:

> It's not just about letting go of thoughts and emotions. It's actually about letting go of the pull that the energy itself has on your consciousness. . . . It sees all of this without thinking about it. . . . It simply watches. . . . All the energies that it watches will just come and go, unless you lose your center of consciousness and go with them. . . .
>
> Don't think you'd be free if you just didn't have these kinds of feelings. It's not true. If you can be free even though you're having these kinds of feelings, then you're really free—because there will always be something.[3]

When you become the observer, you watch your feelings and you don't go with them. You can feel anger, but you don't need to become angry. You can feel annoyed, but you don't need to become annoyed. You can feel jealousy, but you don't need to become jealous. You can feel shame, but you don't need to become ashamed. The trick to having the power to feel your thoughts and feelings without becoming them is to observe them.

Watch the physical reaction your body goes through. Watch the thoughts that come to your mind. Allow yourself to fully feel the emotions that rise. As you do, you'll notice that it passes. Just like a wave. Why? Because your heart remained open. By allowing yourself to fully feel the emotions, they pass on through without you going with them.

Fear is the number one reason we close up. We are afraid of the pain of negative emotions, so in order to protect ourselves from the pain, we close up. Pain is inevitable. Suffering is optional. You will feel pain. If you allow yourself to feel the discomfort, to truly feel it, lean into it, watch it, and observe it, you will be surprised at how quickly it passes. Suffering comes when you close up and embody the very emotions you're fighting to suppress.

Becoming the observer does not mean that you need to psychoanalyze everything. You don't need to figure out why you felt these feelings or why you got triggered. As well intentioned as you may be, now is not the time. Becoming the observer is just watching. That's it. For it is in this objectivity that you allow the emotions to flow through you and let them go.

The most powerful line for me in *The Untethered Soul* is when Michael Singer says, "Nothing, ever, is worth closing your heart over."[4] I'll say it again. "Nothing, ever, is worth closing your heart over." Your false identity will disagree vehemently. Your true identity knows that this is one of the most important truths you can ever learn.

CHANGING HOW YOU FEEL

Clearing Tool #6: Deep Breathing

"I need your verbal consent to perform this procedure. This is a matter of life or death. Do I have your permission?" His voice was unfamiliar to me, but his tone of assertive urgency quickly conveyed the mortal danger of my situation.

I managed a tiny nod, eyes still shut, and quickly focused back on breathing. Inhale, exhale. Inhale, exhale. Someone draped a cover over my face and the procedure began.

In June 2014, twelve hours after having a baby, my body began to seizure with the first stage of nine pulmonary embolisms (blood clots) in my lungs. In such a state, I was aware of nothing else but the frantic need to breathe—a process I rarely think about day to day, yet in these moments breath became a sacred connection to preserving my life on earth. Even with the assistance of twenty liters of oxygen blasting like a fire hose through a mask covering my mouth and nose, breath seemed to be quickly slipping away in ever-increasing restriction.

I was transported from the hospital to an ambulance destined to drive through the canyon to the next town. A rare summer rainstorm had flared suddenly, prohibiting the life flight helicopter from reaching my current location. From there, I would fly to the next hospital, which was better equipped to try to save my life.

The ride was bumpy and uncomfortable, but nothing mattered except those twenty liters of oxygen. When we finally emerged through the canyon to the next town, there was a beautiful interlude from the ambulance to the helicopter, where my body was exposed to the cool night air and the fresh rain falling all around. It felt so peaceful and comforting to have a moment outside the confines of sterile walls. Had I the ability to breathe freely, I would have taken in a brilliant breath. My skin breathed for me, soaking in the freshness of the night and the life-giving energy of the rain.

Voices of urgency hovered above me while cramming my stretcher into a tiny helicopter. My feet pressed tightly against the wall, making me feel too tall for the short space. Hands quickly moved to change over my oxygen to the helicopter supply.

"She needs twenty liters!" the EMT commanded.

"The chopper only has fifteen!" the pilot fired back.

"She needs twenty!" the EMT stated in a panic. My heart sank. Breathing was about to get far more difficult.

The EMT placed the new oxygen mask on my face, and instantly I felt the reduction in air supply. Each breath fighting to receive enough to survive. I gasped. My body was now on high alert. *Please let me breathe! Please give me air!*

"Stay with us, Brooke!" I heard the attendant say at my noticeable fall in responsiveness.

"She needs more air!"

"We don't have it!"

I kept on focusing on my breathing. Inhale. Exhale. I can't breathe! I can't breathe!

"Keep breathing, Brooke! Stay with us!" the voice said again. "We're losing her! We're losing her!" the voice repeated in urgency.

Reality settled in. I knew in that moment there simply wasn't enough. I could not live if I could not breathe. In a sudden flash, a phrase manifested into my mind with radiant clarity. *Christ is the breath of life.* I clung to these words, a lifeline and my last hope of survival.

What began as words boldly declared to my spirit became more powerful as I began to repeat them in my mind with every gasping breath. *Christ is the breath of life.* Inhale. *Christ is the breath of life.* Exhale. Over and over again with devoted focus and a prayerful heart. Moments passed. *Christ is the breath of life.* Inhale. *Christ is the breath of life.* Exhale. *Christ is the breath of life.* Inhale. *Christ is the breath of life.* Exhale.

"She's stabilizing!" the EMT said a few minutes later. "I can't believe it!" In an evanescent moment, I felt the breath of life fill my body. God had restored my life. I was going to live!

The hand of God coupled with the powerful tool of intentional breathing saved my life on that stormy June night. And it has continued to save me ever since. In the years following this experience, I have felt compelled to more fully understand the power of breath, especially breath with mantra—a repeated phrase or word. Yoga and meditation have become invaluable tools for me to deliberately increase the flow in my body and to reconnect my body to the spirit of my true self.

Even in its simplest form, breath holds power to cleanse and restore. Deep breathing cleanses the body of toxins, opens up your organs, relaxes your muscles, processes negative emotions, stabilizes your heart rate, and brings revitalizing energy to your body and your mind.

It is no wonder that such a powerful tool is so readily used throughout the world in every culture and many practices. It is the gateway of life. It is free. And you can use it at any moment. So how do you use it to clear away the false self? Here are a few of my favorite variations:

- **Deep inhales and exhales through the nose:** At first your lung capacity may be limited, especially if you find yourself experiencing a moment of closure from negative thoughts or emotions. Remember your capacity will increase with each repetition. Close your eyes and continue to breathe deep inhales and exhales through your nose. A full minute or two of deep breathing can completely turn your day around and restore you to your true identity.
- **Deep breathing colors:** With eyes closed, breathe deeply through your nose. On the inhale, visualize a soothing color or pure white light filling up

your body. On the exhale, breathe out the color of thoughts or feelings you desire to leave you. Maybe it's murky or black or red. Continue to inhale your soothing color and exhale your toxin color for one to two minutes.

- **Deep breathing words:** With eyes closed, breathe deeply through your nose. On the inhale, pick a word or emotion you desire to inhabit your body, peace, love, calmness. On the exhale, pick a word or emotion you desire to leave your body, anger, embarrassment, sadness.

Clearing Tool #7: Move Your Body: Music, Dance, and Exercise

Exercise has long been touted as an excellent source to release endorphins and de-stress the body. This is a common clearing tool used by many who go for a run, walk, bike, or hit the gym in effort to shake off stress and negative emotions that block us from feeling like our true selves. Moving your body can be a tool used in infinite ways and need not take a huge block of time or special equipment.

In our house, four o'clock usually warrants a much-needed dance party, as we can all be a bit irritable, tired, and hungry in that final stretch before dinner. One afternoon in a moment of near craziness, I grabbed the portable speaker and headed outside to our backyard. To the amazement of the kids, I turned the volume full blast on an energetic song, which I put on repeat, and clambered onto the trampoline. For the next twenty minutes, we all jumped like animals and belted the chorus like fanatic groupies. My kids were ecstatic at the fun, while I clung to the very real need to pump out all my stress and impatience. Quickly abandoned were the bickering and boiling tempers.

To this day, "It's Gonna Be Okay" by The Piano Guys[5] is requested more than any other song, as we all remember the memory of that extraordinary afternoon and more so the incredible elation we experienced in moving our bodies together. Never underestimate the power of a few minutes moving vigorously, especially when paired with uplifting music.

Clearing Tool #8: Emotional Freedom Technique

Emotional Freedom Technique is a simple energy tool performed by firmly tapping with three fingers of one hand along the meridian acupuncture points of your body. The meridian points include the top of your head, brow, side of your eye, under your eye, under your nose, your chin, your collar bone, and under your arm. There are many wonderful YouTube videos that teach the basics, and this tool is quickly learned and quickly executed to clear trapped emotions and limiting beliefs.

I like to imagine that the tapping breaks up the emotion into tiny pieces that can then more easily process through the body and clear. I love having this tool in my toolbox and use it often. For a great resource on EFT, visit www.thetappingsolution.com.

I use this tool regularly on myself and with my kids when they are in a state of heightened emotion or fear. It physiologically calms the body very quickly. As much as I request my kids to take a deep inhale when they are crying and nearly hyperventilating in intense emotion, getting a deep breath out of them can sometimes feel impossible to manage. Tapping on these energy points quickly takes the intensity down to a manageable place.

EFT not only has the ability to clear the physical and emotional symptoms of trapped emotions but also is a powerful tool for clearing limiting beliefs on a mental and spiritual level. Two years after my pulmonary embolisms, I began experiencing intense panic attacks, nightmares, flashbacks, and PTSD. The very sight of a helicopter would transport me back in time and my body would go into a state of panic. EFT Tapping was highly effective for clearing my PTSD, and, gratefully, I can now retell my story and feel only the positive emotions from such a powerful experience and not the many trapped emotions that used to surface upon recall. The ability to now share my experience from a place of wholeness allows me to fully live in my true identity. I can act for myself rather than be acted upon from the emotions and traumas of my past.

EFT TAPPING POINTS

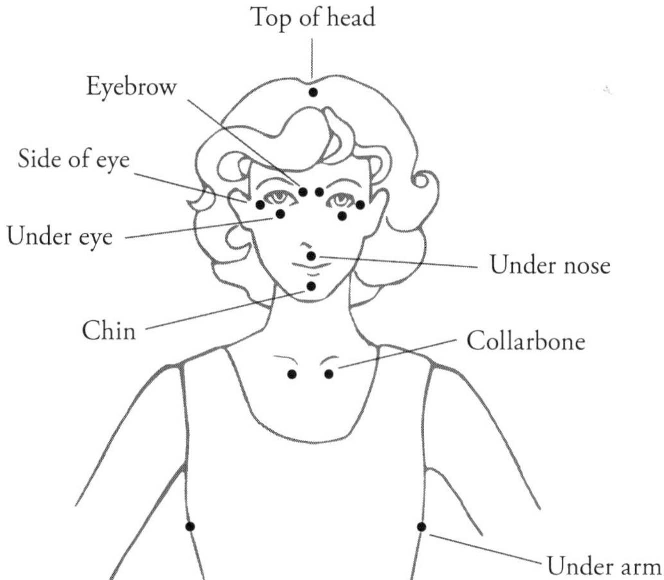

Clearing Tool #9: Forgiveness

Several years ago, in the glow of a campfire, I listened to this profound story:

> Two monks were traveling to the top of a mountain. Along the way they encountered a stream where an old woman was standing on the bank.
>
> "Carry me across!" she eagerly demanded. "For I cannot cross on my own."
>
> The wise monk lifted her upon his back and waded into the water. He gently carried her for several minutes before reaching the other side.
>
> "Put me down!" the woman commanded, and the wise monk gently let her down. "Do you have any food?" she asked. "I'm hungry." The monk opened his sack and generously took out two thick slices of bread and some cheese and gave it to the woman before continuing on his way.
>
> As the two monks traveled the mountain road, the younger monk steamed inside.
>
> *How could that woman be so rude?* he thought. *She was so ungrateful! She did not even thank my friend for carrying her through the water and giving her of his food!*
>
> These thoughts plagued him for several hours as he followed behind his friend, who walked onward in silence. No longer able to stay quiet, he voiced his troubled thoughts aloud. The wise monk listened quietly then turned to his young friend and said, "I put the woman down several hours ago. Why are you still carrying her?"[6]

This wasn't the ending I was expecting. I had felt many of the same accusations as the young monk. Yet, in a profound and simple statement, the wise monk acknowledged offensive things do happen in life, but we lighten our load when we choose to no longer carry them.

Desmund Tutu writes in *The Book of Forgiveness*:

> Our nature is goodness. Yes, we do much that is bad, but our essential nature is good. If it were not, then we would not be shocked and dismayed when we harm one another. When someone does something ghastly, it makes the news because it is the exception to the rule. We live surrounded by so much love, kindness, and trust that we forget it is remarkable. Forgiveness is the way we return what has been taken from us and restore the love and kindness and trust that has been lost. With each act of forgiveness, whether small or great, we move toward wholeness.[7]

Moving toward wholeness is moving toward your own divine nature. Harboring resentment, hurt, and pain against another veils your true identity. Forgiveness reconnects you to your true self and restores your ability to see the true identity in others.

Seek for ways to free yourself from carrying those who have hurt you. Many of the tools we have outlined here can assist in the practice of forgiveness. In the simplest form, forgiveness involves the same three elements of creation: how we see, say, and feel toward another person. To forgive, we must see others differently, speak differently, and feel differently. In chapter 10, we will learn how to see others in their true identity. For when we see the truth in others, we will see the truth in ourselves. For we are all connected in our humanity.

Clearing Tool #10: The Redeeming and Enabling Power of Jesus Christ

Eustace Scrubb is a character in the C. S. Lewis novel *The Voyage of the Dawn Treader.* Eustace is a spoiled, selfish boy who finds himself in possession of a large fortune. Seduced by the thoughts of a life of comfort and luxury, he falls asleep with his treasure. When he wakes, Eustace discovers he is no longer the boy he was before.

> He had turned into a dragon while he was asleep. Sleeping on a dragon's hoard with greedy, dragonish thoughts in his heart, he had become a dragon himself.[8]

Eustace spends several days in a miserable struggle. How can he turn into a boy again? Finally, in his most desperate moment of despair, he begins to peel off the dragon skin. Impassioned by the thoughts of freeing himself from his captivity, he peels off layer upon layer of skin, but in his exhausted dismay, he discovers it is all in vain. He is still a dragon.

> "You will have to let me undress you," [says Aslan the Lion]. I was afraid of his claws, I can tell you, but I was pretty nearly desperate now. So I just lay flat down on my back to let him do it.
>
> The very first tear he made was so deep that I thought it had gone right into my heart. And when he began pulling the skin off, it hurt worse than anything I've ever felt. The only thing that made me able to bear it was just the pleasure of feeling the stuff peel off. . . .
>
> Well, he peeled the beastly stuff right off. . . . And there was I as smooth and soft as a peeled switch and smaller than I had been. Then he caught hold of me—I didn't like that much for I was very tender underneath now that I'd no skin on—and threw me into the water. It smarted like anything but only for a moment. After that it became perfectly delicious and as soon as I started swimming and splashing I found that all the pain had gone from my arm. And then I saw why. I'd turned into a boy again. . . .
>
> After a bit the lion took me out and dressed me . . . in new clothes.[9]

The false identity indeed can feel like dragon skin, a beastly façade of who you really are. Fully shedding the skin is ultimately an act of grace from Jesus Christ. It is He that holds the power to save you from an eternity as a dragon and to redeem you to your divine nature.

"For the natural man is an enemy to God, and has been from the fall of Adam, and will be, forever and ever, unless he yields to the enticings of the Holy Spirit, and putteth off the natural man and becometh a saint through the atonement of Christ the Lord" (Mosiah 3:19).

Every tool for clearing the false identity is empowered by the redeeming power of Jesus Christ. Try as you may to shed your dragon skin relying upon your efforts alone, it is His power that lasts and reaches to the very depths of your heart. Even after you finally break free, the life ahead requires a close friendship to your Redeemer to continually free you again and again as it requires practice to stay in and develop your divine nature.

As such, I am comforted by the following words in the conclusion of Eustace's story.

> It would be nice, and fairly nearly true, to say that "from that time forth Eustace was a different boy." To be strictly accurate, he began to be a different boy. He had relapses. There were still many days when he could be very tiresome. But most of those I shall not notice. The cure had begun.[10]

The Redeeming and Enabling Power of Christ's Atonement

Elder David A. Bednar taught that the Atonement of Jesus Christ embodies both a redeeming power and an enabling power. The redeeming power of the Atonement redeems us from our false identity, and the enabling power enables us to develop into our true identity, or as Elder Bednar says:

> The redeeming and enabling powers of the Atonement are . . . connected and complementary; they both need to be operational during all phases of the journey of life. And it is eternally important for all of us to recognize that *both* of these essential elements of the journey of mortality—both putting off the natural man and becoming a saint, both overcoming bad and becoming good—are accomplished through the power of the Atonement.[11]

King Benjamin gives a remarkable map to this process. "For the natural man is an enemy to God, and has been from the fall of Adam, and will be, forever and ever, unless he yields to the enticings of the Holy Spirit, and putteth off the natural man and becometh a saint through the atonement of Christ the Lord (Mosiah 3:19). Let's break his words down:

"For the natural man is an enemy to God"

This natural man identity is an enemy to God, because it is false. It is not who God created you to be.

"And has been from the fall of Adam, and will be, forever and ever"

Just as we saw in chapter 2, the influence of Satan creates a false identity of who we really are. He is allowed to tempt us and try us. He is allowed to say things to our mind, to persuade us to believe we are not a divine son or daughter of God.

When Moses had his divine vision of the creation of the world and speaks with God face to face, the Lord uses this sacred moment to also instruct Moses in his identity. He addresses him in these words, "Moses, thou art my son" (Moses 1:4). Moses feels the glory of God upon him, and is further told, "I have a work for thee, my son" (vs. 6). Not only does the Lord reveal to Moses his true identity as a son of God but He also instructs him in his individual mission upon the earth.

Afterward, Satan appears to Moses. He cunningly and immediately targets Moses's identity through repeatedly referring to him as "Moses, son of man" (Moses 1:12). Just as he did with Adam and Eve, Satan presents a false identity in opposition to the true identity of Moses, and he likewise presents a false identity in opposition to each of us. This is Satan's pattern, and it will always be so.

"Unless he yields to the enticings of the Holy Spirit"

Thankfully, Satan is not the only one who speaks to our mind and heart to tell us who we are. We are also enticed with words of truth from the Holy Spirit. The Holy Spirit speaks of our divine nature, calling us sons and daughters of God. The Holy Spirit speaks of our own unique mission and work we are to accomplish here upon the earth. Yet we cannot develop our true identity unless we yield to Him. We must listen and obey the words that come from the Holy Spirit to our soul.

Learning to discern between these two different voices is imperative to our success. Knowing that God gives us weakness (see Ether 12:27), it can sometimes feel confusing to understand what voice is speaking truth. I have long appreciated the words of my friend Lewis Munday, who said, "The Lord does not tell us what we are not, but what we are. He shows us how far we have come and although he also shows us how far we have to go, and what we can improve, that comes with a feeling of hope, a desire to improve, and a feeling of achievability."

The enabling power of the Atonement of Jesus Christ orients us to who we are. Satan orients us to who we are not. Despite the gap that exists between where we are now and where we hope to be, the enticings of the Holy Spirit are always filled with hope, faith, love, and peace.

In learning to discern these influences, it is important to recall that the voice we feed and heed is the voice that will be the strongest. Just like the two wolves, as we learn obedience to the Holy Spirit, the voice of God grows clearer and stronger in our life.

CLEARING TOOL #11: CALL UPON GOD AND COMMAND SATAN TO DEPART

"PUTTETH OFF THE NATURAL MAN"

Webster's 1828 dictionary defines "put-off" as "to degrade; to deprive of authority, power or place. To confute; to silence."[12] When we put off the false identity of the natural man, we deprive Satan of authority, power, and place in our life. We silence the words and influence he has upon our nature. We take back our agency and act for ourselves instead of being acted upon.

Though we are each endowed with the gift of agency, the use of agency is limited or liberated, according to our choices. Lehi taught, "Wherefore, men are free according to the flesh. . . . And they are free to choose liberty and eternal life, through the great Mediator of all men, or to choose captivity and death, according to the captivity and power of the devil; for he seeketh that all men might be miserable like unto himself" (2 Nephi 2:27).

The natural man identity is bondage to who you really are. We feel this bondage when we sin and can be freed through repentance and the redeeming power of the Atonement of Christ. We can also feel this bondage when Satan is in our presence. When Joseph Smith went to the grove to pray, he describes his encounter with Satan in these words:

> I kneeled down and began to offer up the desires of my heart to God. I had scarcely done so, when immediately I was seized upon by some power which entirely overcame me, and had such an astonishing influence over me as to bind my tongue so that I could not speak. Thick darkness gathered around me, and it seemed to me for a time as if I were doomed to sudden destruction. (Joseph Smith History 1:15)

There are times in our lives even when we are acting in righteous obedience that we feel the power and influence of the adversary binding us from the light of our true identity. We can feel helpless and bound. Joseph shows us how to put off the natural man in these moments. He continues saying:

> But, exerting all my powers to *call upon God to deliver me out of the power of this enemy which had seized upon me*, and at the very moment when I was ready to sink into despair and abandon myself to destruction—not to an imaginary ruin, but to the power of some actual being from the unseen world, who had such marvelous power as I had never before felt in any being—just at this moment of great alarm, I saw a pillar of light exactly over my head, above the brightness of the sun, which descended gradually until it fell upon me.
>
> It no sooner appeared than *I found myself delivered from the enemy which held me bound.* (Joseph Smith—History 1:16–17, emphasis added)

Moses too when confronted by Satan needed to find a way to be delivered. Despite Satan's lies to Moses regarding his identity, Moses recognizes the difference between how it feels to be in the glory of God's presence and in the presence of Satan. He says:

> His glory has been upon me, wherefore I can judge between him and thee. *Depart hence, Satan.*
>
> And now, when Moses had said these words, Satan cried with a loud voice, and ranted upon the earth, and commanded, saying: I am the Only Begotten, worship me.
>
> And it came to pass that Moses began to fear exceedingly; and as he began to fear, he saw the bitterness of hell. Nevertheless, *calling upon God, he received strength, and he commanded, saying: Depart from me, Satan,* for this one God only will I worship, which is the God of glory.
>
> And now Satan began to tremble, and the earth shook; and Moses received strength, and *called upon God, saying: In the name of the Only Begotten, depart hence, Satan.*
>
> And it came to pass that Satan cried with a loud voice, with weeping, and wailing, and gnashing of teeth; and he departed hence, even from the presence of Moses, that he beheld him not. (Moses 1:18–22, emphasis added)

Days ago, I had the impression I needed to write more about Satan in my book. My first draft scarcely mentioned him, and yet he is the source of the false identity. Satan has greater power when he remains anonymous. Naming him, convicting him for his crimes, and identifying him as the source of our false identity bring us great freedom. Doing this shines a light into the darkness. Like Moses, we begin to see the difference between the glory of who God created us to be and the identity Satan presents with no glory.

No sooner had I resolved to revise my book that I suddenly came under a great depression. For a whole day, I felt a dark shadow hovering upon me. I went about my day—which included a wonderful family adventure together—but despite the event, I felt a deep sadness and inability to function in my true identity of happiness and joy. By the end of the day, I finally connected the dots and asked my husband for a priesthood blessing to help free me from this bondage.

There is power in calling upon God for deliverance. There is power in commanding Satan to depart in the name of Jesus Christ. This is a very real application of putting off the natural man and personifying the infinite power of the Atonement of Jesus Christ.

"And becometh a saint through the Atonement of Christ the Lord"

I love the beauty of this imagery. Becoming a saint requires the highest level of devotion and development. It is preparatory to fully realize who you are created to become. This supreme development is only possible through the Atonement of

Jesus Christ. Putting off the natural man is only possible through the Atonement of Jesus Christ.

Both the redeeming and enabling powers of the Savior work together in magnificence to free us from all that is false and transform us into gods and goddesses. Truly, He created us in His own image, to ultimately become as He is (see Genesis 1:26).

Becoming a saint is the process of continually putting off the natural man and continually learning to yield to the Holy Spirit. You must be redeemed over and over again from your sins and enabled continually to develop the Christ-like character and attributes that are within, for this is who you really are. This is your true identity.

Journal Questions

1. Do you have your own clearing tool you use for negative thoughts and emotions? What is it?
2. What new tool do you think would be most helpful for you to try?

Notes

1. See this study discussed in Marc Berman, "Bermon on the Brain: How to Boost Your Focus," *Huffpost*, February 2, 2012, https://www.huffingtonpost.ca/marc-berman/attention-restoration-theory-nature_b_1242261.html.
2. Attributed to Viktor Frankl.
3. Michael A. Singer, *The Untethered Soul: The Journey Beyond Yourself.* (Oakland: New Harbinger Publications, 2007), 64, 66.
4. Ibid., 47.
5. Al van der Beek, vocalist, "Okay," written by Andy Grammar and Dave Basset, The Piano Guys arrangement produced by Al van der Beek and Steven Sharp Nelson, track 4 on *Uncharted*, 2016.
6. See a similar telling of this story in Ray Roberts, *God Confidence: A Practical Guide for Reaching the Divine Zone* (Bloomington: Balboa Press, 2014) 66.
7. Desmond Tutu and Mpho Tutu, *The Book of Forgiving: The Fourfold Path for Healing Ourselves and Our World*, (London: HarperCollins UK, 2014), iii.
8. C. S. Lewis, *The Voyage of the Dawn Treader*, The Chronicles of Narnia (New York: HarperCollins Publishers, 1980) 96.
9. Ibid., 115–17.
10. Ibid., 119–20.
11. David A. Bednar, "The Atonement and the Journey of Mortality," *Ensign*, Apr. 2012.
12. *American Dictionary of the English Language* (1828), s.v. "put-off."

Chapter 5

Getting to Know the True Self

NATURE AND TRUE IDENTITY

What color is a carrot? Did you know carrots come in many colors and varieties? Have you ever eaten a purple carrot? Pure delight awaits you as you crunch into its flesh to reveal a stunning yellow center! The variety and detail in God's creations are truly endless.

He didn't limit His creation of the carrot to one variety—he created many. He didn't stop with one variety of tree or plant. There are countless varieties. He didn't stop with one variety of man or woman. Humans are God's greatest creation of all, and no man or woman is like any other.

The various vegetation in the world is perfectly matched with the right climate. A tall palm tree thrives in the hot desert in Southern California, yet doesn't survive the harsh cold winter in Alberta, Canada. The pine tree will hold onto its green needles all winter long, yet the maple tree's leaves turn color and fall off when autumn approaches.

How silly it would be for a pine tree to despair that her needles never turned color or fell off. How silly it would be for the apple tree to gaze at a redwood tree and wonder why she wasn't as tall. God placed every tree and plant in the climate specific to its growth. God designed every living thing with unique qualities, different shapes, colors, and sizes, and amazing detail.

And here we are as humans, often comparing ourselves and our lives to someone else, convinced we should be different than we are. Perhaps we are a steady ponderosa pine tree looking longingly at a red maple wishing we could change color. Perhaps we are an oak tree gazing covetously at the blue spruce midwinter, wishing our branches were not bare for the season.

Nature is content and glorifies God in filling the measure of her creation. We will only find true happiness when we can do the same. When you know the details of what makes you unique and wonderful, it's much easier to be content and rejoice in who you are.

YOU ARE A SEED

God created you to be your own unique variety. You come to earth with a perfect identity. Just like a seed, you have all potential coded inside you. He plants you in the specific climate and conditions He knows you need to grow and to ultimately thrive. Your seed is pure and perfect. It's whole. You have perfect potential to become exactly who God designed you to become. When you begin the process of clearing away your false identity, what you find is the seed of who you are. It has always been there, it was always good, and it was always whole.

The worth of a seed is inherent. Your worth is not based upon how tall you can grow or whether you can survive a cold winter. Your worth is not based upon how many other trees look up to you. Your worth is not even based upon how much fruit you produce. The precise reason a farmer plants a seed is because he knows the worth it holds within. He has faith it will grow. He envisions the vast potential that will pour forth in its cultivation and the contribution it will bring to the world.

You are the same. Your worth and potential are always within you, and further yet, you are eternal. You may be living in a mortal body now, but your spirit and potential were created long before coming to earth, and they will continue to exist in eternity after this life.

True to the pattern of all God's creations, you too are unique and amazing. Inside you, He has created someone like no other. You have a perfectly unique makeup of characteristics, personality, attributes, interests, desires, talents, hopes, dreams, influence, and purpose unlike anyone else in the world.

THE TRUTH ABOUT PERFECTION

I have used the word "perfect" several times in reference to your true identity. It's a trigger word for some, and depending on your relationship with perfectionism, you may or may not have some discomfort in its use.

God commanded "be ye therefore perfect" (Matthew 5:48). However, the word "perfect" does not currently retain the same meaning it did two thousand years ago. The original Hebrew and Greek interpretation means "to be whole and complete."

Our modern day understanding of "perfect" changed in the Industrial Revolution in the 1890s. Machines were introduced into the world and suddenly there was a new association. "Perfect" now became "flawless," as machines could mass produce with greater precision. This modern-world understanding of perfect has created the belief that our value is tied to performance—a flawless one. That our value is tied to an end product, a point of arrival. Add this modern definition on top of God's commandment to be perfect, and you get unrealistic expectations and pressure.

Remember, Jesus commanded us to *be* perfect. He did not command us to *do* perfect. He is inviting us to be *whole* and to be *complete. Be* the true you! With His redeeming and enabling power, you become whole and complete. With His power, you clear away the false identity and find the whole, complete, "perfect" self He created.

THE PURPOSE OF OUR LIFE IS TO DEVELOP AND GROW

Modern-day perfectionism demands that you be seen or perform above the human condition. Such a notion is an immature understanding of life. Life is not flawless. People are not flawless. There are many things you are, and there are many things you have the potential to become.

You are a seed, and a seed must develop and grow. Your true identity is in development, and, as such, you have the responsibility to work together with the Lord to cultivate who you are now into who God created you to be.

Development becomes much more enjoyable when you stop demanding a flawless performance. Personal growth can be grim and unbearable when attempted from within the false identity. Perfectionism, unrealistic expectations, shaming yourself for slow progress or for making mistakes, or even allowing the incentive of competition to fuel your development to secure validation from others, is a surefire way to crash and burn.

Remember our earlier description of a new baby? She loves herself and loves others and embodies her divine nature. Because she exists in this state of love, she will learn and progress at a rapid pace. Your growth and development likewise speed up when you work on it from within your true identity; when you treat yourself with love and compassion, when you receive and give grace and forgiveness to yourself, when you enjoy the process of growth and all the new adventures it brings.

Who wouldn't want a more enjoyable, sustainable, fast-paced approach to developing who you really are? As you come to accept the original meaning of "perfect," and live life in your true identity, everything falls into its natural place. When you stumble, you dust yourself off and happily try again. You are no longer the one holding yourself back.

GETTING TO KNOW YOUR TRUE IDENTITY

Just as the adversary will entice you to create a false identity through influencing how you see, what you say, and how you feel, the Holy Spirit will entice you to discover your true identity in the same pattern of creation.

How You See in Your True Identity

You see yourself with compassion. You see others with compassion. You see your potential. You see the potential and true identity of others, even when they're not living it. You see your worth as inherent. You see life through the lens of faith and possibility. You find evidence of God's blessings all around you. You see humanity as your fellow brothers and sisters.

The Words of Your True Identity

I am enough! I can! I belong. I have everything I need. I am loved. I love others. Life is working out for me. I forgive you. I am safe. I am whole. I am okay. I am united. I am not alone. I am one. I am supported. I am surrounded by help. Life is easy. I am working together with others. I am working together with God.

Feelings of Your True Identity

- peace
- joy
- forgiveness
- contentment
- gratitude
- love
- understanding
- compassion
- empathy
- motivation
- ambition
- enthusiasm
- faith
- hope
- delight
- dedication
- discipline
- order
- confidence
- strength
- commitment
- patience
- optimism
- respect

When you feel negative emotions in your true identity, your heart remains open. The true identity allows emotion to flow through you without you going with it. You may feel anger, but you don't become anger. You feel envy without becoming envy. You feel impatient without becoming impatient. You allow yourself to feel all emotion without closing and, therefore, retain your ability to act for yourself without being acted upon. You are proactive rather than reactive.

This is what it means to be long suffering. To suffer, means "to allow." You allow the feelings to pass through you, but you are not easily provoked by them (see Moroni 7:45).

David gives an inspiring description of the Lord's feelings, including the negative emotion of anger: "The Lord is gracious, and full of compassion; slow to anger, and of great mercy" (Psalm 145:8). The Lord is slow to anger. He is not reactive, rather, He wisely chooses how to respond to His children in a perfect balance of justice and mercy. Know that within the seed of your true identity, you too are encoded with this ability. It takes practice to not close your heart or react when negative emotions surface. As you develop your true identity, you too will grow in openness and be slow to close your heart.

If this description of your true identity doesn't represent your life at all times, take heart! We are all working toward living in our true identity more often than not. This is why we need the redeeming and enabling power of the Atonement of Jesus Christ daily in our life. Knowing that this description is who you really are invokes courage to repent and try again. Living in your true identity is the only path to peace and happiness because you are living in alignment with who you really are.

DISCOVERING YOUR TRUE SELF

Your Own Variety

Your true identity is a place of peace and potential and includes the general description of what I just outlined. Additionally, you have a unique combination of details that make you distinctly you. This is already apparent in your physical features and DNA. It also exists in your spiritual features and spiritual DNA. This includes your interests, desires, attributes, hopes, dreams, spiritual gifts, natural talents, yet-to-be developed talents, and your mission and purpose.

One of the exciting adventures of life is discovering your own unique qualities and developing your identity. This is an eternal process, one that began in the premortal life before you came to earth and continues into eternity after this life. With a veil of forgetfulness blocking the memory of your life before, you spend a good portion of time here relearning who you are and experiencing trials and opportunities that are specially designed to help you grow.

As part of this discovery process, let's explore a few key areas that give insight into who you are individually.

Your Roles versus Attributes

Roles are associated with your relationships and commitments in your life. Roles provide opportunities for growth and development. They can also be seasonal and evolve throughout your life.

When you build your identity on a role, you risk losing your identity. I have known many women who build their identities on their role as mothers, only to feel lost in meeting the demands of those they serve or to struggle to know who they are when their nests become empty.

When I left an eight-year career as a professional photographer, I lost confidence in who I was because I had identified my role of photographer with my sense of worth. It's easy to fall into the snare of identifying with your roles, and, culturally, we tend to promote it. When someone asks you to tell them about yourself, how do you usually respond? Most commonly, we list our roles! I am a mother, a wife, a podcaster, an entrepreneur. Roles are good and necessary to your life, but your roles are not who you are. Your roles are what you do. Most people never learn to discern between the two, and when the roles change, or you don't perform in that role to the level of your expectation, your personal worth can feel challenged. Instead, you must learn who you are *within* your role.

We speak of roles as the hats we wear. When I wear the hat of motherhood, I bring attributes of organization, structure, perfecting, simplicity, and inspiration. When my sister wears the hat of motherhood, she brings the attributes of playfulness, imagination, humor, spontaneity, and adventure. We wear the hats differently and uniquely.

If I look at the way she wears her hat and think I should be a lot more playful and adventurous in my role as mother, it's akin to me being a pine tree and looking at the red maple wondering why my needles don't change color. In my comparison, I'm totally overlooking the strong attributes I bring that make me unique.

Now, berating myself that I should be more playful and adventurous is not the same as setting a goal to develop these attributes myself. Nonetheless, playfulness is going to look different in a pine tree than it does in a red maple tree. Whatever attributes I have or develop will still express in their own unique way.

If you feel like you have ever lost yourself in your roles, this next exercise will be particularly helpful. When you can identify your attributes, you effectively bring your true identity into your role.

Your Roles

Fill in the blank for the following statement ten times.

"I am a ______________________________."
"I am a ______________________________."
"I am a ______________________________."
"I am a ______________________________."
"I am a ______________________________."
"I am a ______________________________."
"I am a ______________________________."
"I am a ______________________________."
"I am a ______________________________."
"I am a ______________________________."

Your Attributes

Watch what happens when we eliminate one word. "I am __________."

Grammatically, you can no longer fill in the blank with your roles. What are your options now? Your attributes! Now complete the new statement ten times:

"I am ______________________________."
"I am ______________________________."
"I am ______________________________."
"I am ______________________________."
"I am ______________________________."
"I am ______________________________."
"I am ______________________________."
"I am ______________________________."
"I am ______________________________."
"I am ______________________________."

This simple distinction beautifully demonstrates how your true identity is embodied in your unique attributes. Your true identity is not your roles or past achievements. It's the attributes you have and the attributes you develop that flavor everything you do. It is who you are *inside* your role.

You will grow in your ability to see and develop your attributes. These statements are a powerful way to discover who you really are and also a powerful way to further your development. We will talk in greater detail about this in the following chapter.

YOUR TALENTS AND SPIRITUAL GIFTS

Dallin H. Oaks stated, "We should seek after spiritual gifts. They can lead us to God. They can shield us from the power of the adversary. They can compensate for our inadequacies and repair our imperfections."[1] You have unique talents and spiritual gifts. Some of these may already be obvious to you, and other gifts may take some careful searching. Remember, your gifts and talents are inside you, not outside you.

When I left a budding music career to serve a mission for eighteen months, I felt a distinct loss in my identity from leaving the stage and the piano. I felt those two objects were important for people to know who I was. I struggled without them, wanting the comfort and validation they provided for me. But a stage and piano are not part of me. They are outside of me. As is a soccer ball, microphone, sewing machine, paint brush, camera, pen and paper, or any other number of things we may associate as our gift or talent.

My talent was not a piano or a stage, in the same vein that you are not your roles. If I looked deeper, I would have found that my talent was really the attributes of musicality, focus, dedication, and discipline. Had I been able to distinguish my true talents as they exist inside of me, being separated from a piano and stage would have not triggered the identity crisis it did. I could have instead found new ways to apply these talents to my current environment and season of life.

Culturally, we lean toward thinking about talents in an external sense. Those who don't shine with the arts or a sport often concede to believing they have no talent at all. The following exercise is helpful in identifying talents that may be less obvious—because they aren't naturally linked to external objects or activities. Talents such as enthusiasm, listening to others, making peace, making friends, hospitality, vision, teaching, organization, compassion, optimism, creative ideas, and problem-solving are a few examples. Chances are you have far more talents and special gifts than you originally thought. Learning to recognize the talents and gifts inside you will expand the possibilities of how you use and share them.

My Gifts and Talents Inside Me

List your talents that connect to objects. Let's look at these talents. Can you identify a spiritual gift that fuels that talent? A spiritual gift is an attribute and quality that you always carry within you and that you can express in ways beyond objects or tools. Here are a few examples of talents within: creativity, love, focus, discipline, dedication, idea generating, problem solving, optimism, humor, listening, faith, hope, vision, gentleness, empathy, compassion, organization, planning, leadership, courage, charity, making art, and loyalty. Now, list your own qualities or attributes.

TALENTS THAT CONNECT TO OBJECTS (i.e., playing the piano)	*SPIRITUAL GIFTS THAT FUEL TALENTS INSIDE ME* (focus, dedication, discipline, etc.)

YOUR DESIRES AND CURIOSITY

Pay attention to your desires. What lights you up? What brings you joy? What are you curious about? Do you always read books on a very particular topic? Do you have a burning desire to learn all you can about a certain subject? Do you have dreams about pursuing a particular adventure? What are your desires? List these desires.

EXPERTISE

Pay attention to what people come to you for. What do they ask your advice on or ask your help with? Consider big things and small things and list them as well.

Ask Others

Many times, we do not recognize these qualities that exist inside of ourselves because we don't practice seeing them. Asking someone who knows you well is a brave and exhilarating exercise in learning more about yourself. Choose three to five people you love and trust to describe the attributes and gifts that they see within you. Consider your spouse, parents, siblings, children, friends, and teachers. When you gather their responses, look for patterns. Do you see anything repeated? Record their responses.

Ask God

God knows you better than anyone else. Special direction given in patriarchal blessings or other priesthood blessings can also be a sacred source to learn more about your own divine gifts and mission. Ask the Lord in prayer to help you see what your gifts are. Pay close attention to words or impressions that come to your mind or that show up for you in the following few days. Record any impressions.

Note

1. Dallin H. Oaks, "Spiritual Gifts," *Ensign*, Sept. 1986.

Chapter 6

Empowering the True Self

ALL ABOUT LOVE

Master, which is the great commandment in the law? Jesus said unto him, Thou shalt love the Lord thy God with all thy heart, and with all thy soul, and with all thy mind. This is the first and great commandment. And the second is like unto it, Thou shalt love thy neighbor as thyself. On these two commandments hang all the law and the prophets" (Matthew 22:36–40).

Can you imagine asking Jesus which of all the commandments was the greatest and most important? Imagine what it must have been like to stand in the crowd of disciples that day and hear this question posed. Surely, we would await His response with alert attention, for there are so many commandments and teachings of how to live your life. To know which principle is the most important would simplify everything. You could ensure that you were, in the very least, doing what was most valuable and of top priority. You could focus on one thing. A list full of things would be much harder.

How does Christ respond? Jesus beautifully synthesizes the entire gospel into one principle that will have the greatest impact upon your life: love. First, to love God. Second, to love your neighbor as yourself. I find it interesting that this second commandment so inextricably connects both neighbor and oneself. He does not say, "Love your neighbor *and* love yourself." Rather, he says, "Love your neighbor *as* yourself." The love we have for our neighbors and the love we have for ourselves are linked. Bound. Connected. There is not one without the other.

The dictionary defines the word "as" to mean "to the same degree or amount."[1] In this symbiotic relationship, we must give equal love to both our neighbors and ourselves.

How well do you love yourself? How well do you love your neighbor? For many, we do better at loving our neighbor, yet we are commanded to do both to the same degree. They are not separate, yet how often do we separate ourselves from this equation?

When you love yourself, right where you are, right in the middle of your development, your whole life changes. If you only remember one thing about your true identity, remember your true identity is love. You were made by love and for love so that you can give love.

The false identity presents the polarity. The false identity is criticism. The most important thing you can ever do for yourself is to never, ever, ever be critical of yourself. *Ever.*

If this is a habit for you, stop it! Immediately! If you can replace self-criticism with self-love, everything else in your life will work out.

Love is the foundation of everything. When God reveals what two commandments are the greatest, we best listen. When God says that all other commandments hang upon these two, he has just revealed the secret to everything.

What does it mean for all other commandments to hang upon these two? The 1828 Webster dictionary defines "hang" as "to depend; to rest on something for support."[2] Everything else in life rests upon love for support. It's the foundation. And loving yourself is an inextricable part of that foundation. Without a foundation, you fall. You fail. You can't progress. Whatever goal you have in life, whatever desire or hope or dream you want to see come forth, it rests here. It cannot be built without a foundation.

Do you want better relationships? Do you want to develop a skill or talent? Do you want to lose weight or get fit? Do you want better health? Do you want financial freedom? Do you want to overcome a weakness? Do you want freedom from any form of addiction? Do you want more joy and happiness? Working on these areas of development from a place of self-love will change everything about the process of growing. Just like the baby who happily keeps trying again in effort to learn to walk and talk, we must learn to deeply love ourselves in order to progress.

The false identity is brimming with criticism and shame, making any effort to develop and improve feel discouraging and hard. The true identity is compassionate, forgiving, and tries again and again with peace and faith. You cannot afford to be self-critical. You must do all you can to truly love you. So how in the world do you reach a place of self-love? How do you get there? It all starts with creation.

THE LAW OF CREATION

As we learned earlier, the pattern of everything that you create in your life, both positive and negative is See + Say + Feel → Actions → Results. Let's break down this equation: If you have a thought in your mind (say), the thought creates an image (see). The words and image together then create a feeling. How you feel influences your actions, and actions bring results. The see-say-feel pattern is completely symbiotic. You can target any one of these three factors and influence the other two.

The Creator Himself teaches this pattern, and we can find each element in the account of the creation of the world.

See

> And every plant of the field before it was in the earth, and every herb of the field before it grew. For I, the Lord God, created all things, of which I have spoken, spiritually, before they were naturally upon the face of the earth. (Moses 3:5)

The Lord creates all things spiritually before he creates them physically. How do you create something spiritually first? You must see it. Spiritual creation begins as a seed in the mind, as a simple thought or vision. That seed begins to grow as plans are made and details fill in the bigger picture.

Think about the amount of detail God must have created spiritually before the physical creation. Think of the sun. He would have already planned exactly how hot it should be, what elements and chemicals it would be made of, exactly how far away it should be from each planet, and so much more. The spiritual creation is what guides the physical. God *sees* it first.

We also create spiritually before we create physically. We build houses from blueprints. We draw a picture based on an image in our mind. We work on a goal with a picture in our head of what we hope to achieve. Spiritual creation always precedes the physical. We must see it.

Say

What does God *say* in the creation process? Perhaps this is the most famous part of the story. Every single detail of the creation account is prefaced by these words, "And God *said*." "And God said, Let there be light: and there was light" (Genesis 1:3). "And God said, Let the waters under the heaven be gathered together unto one place, and let the dry land appear; and it was so" (Genesis 1:9). "And God said, Let us make man in our image, after our likeness" (Genesis 1:26). God's word is power. What He says, He creates.

The Apostle John details this further in his own commentary on the creation, saying, "In the beginning was the Word, and the Word was with God, and the Word was God. All things were made by him; and without him was not any thing made that was made" (John 1:1, 3). God speaks, and it is done. Likewise, the words we speak create. We will explore this is detail when I talk about using words of affirmation.

Feel

Do the Lord's feelings play into the creation process? Absolutely. After each stage of creation, we learn how God feels about it. "And God said, Let there be light: and there was light. And God saw the light, that it was good" (Genesis 1:3–4). He sees it. He says it. He feels it.

The feelings of God are so deeply rooted that they are part of His divine nature. Prophets for thousands of years have described God by describing His feelings. "God is love" (1 John 4:8). "For his merciful kindness is great toward us" (Psalm 117:2). "And his name shall be called Wonderful, Counsellor, The mighty God, The everlasting Father, The Prince of Peace" (Isaiah 9:6). "The fruit of the Spirit is love, joy, peace, longsuffering, gentleness, goodness, faith" (Galatians 5:22).

The Apostle Peter describes how we too can develop the same attributes in God's divine nature. He says, "Whereby are given unto us exceeding great and precious promises: that by these ye might be partakers of the divine nature. . . . And beside this, giving all diligence, add to your faith virtue; and to virtue knowledge; And to knowledge temperance; and to temperance patience; and to patience godliness; And to godliness brotherly kindness; and to brotherly kindness charity. For if these things be in you, and abound, they make you that ye shall neither be barren nor unfruitful in the knowledge of our Lord Jesus Christ" (2 Peter 1:4–8). To know God, as Peter tells us, we must cultivate the feelings of God. And how do we cultivate feelings? Through the way we see and what we say.

YOU ARE A CREATOR

Truly, the Lord is our exemplar in creating. He has shown us His own pattern so we too may create all that is good. This seems so simple. Just choose your thoughts, choose your words, and choose your feelings, and then you are set on the perfect path. Yet this world is one of opposition. We are enticed regularly by both the good and the evil. Additionally, we are creatures of habit. The way we see and what we say have long been practiced, even when we are not consciously thinking about it.

The law of creation holds the power you have to intentionally create your life. When you understand that you are not a victim to your circumstances, you take back your power and begin to create the life you truly desire. If you desire to create a loving relationship with yourself, you must change the way you see yourself and what you say about yourself. This will change your feelings and ultimately your actions and results. You are a creator. You must also become a better one. Let's begin with choosing the best words you can to create your life.

Empowerment Tool #1: Affirmations

God did not create the world by accident or on autopilot. Yet, do we ever create on autopilot? If you don't create on purpose—intentionally feeding your mind with good—the false identity will do it for you. If you want to change your feelings, you need only change what you say and see. Affirmations automatically trigger both.

Louise Hay stated, "An affirmation opens the door. It's a beginning point on the path to change. In essence, you're saying to your subconscious mind: 'I am taking responsibility. I am aware that there is something I can do to change.' When

I talk about *doing affirmations*, I mean consciously choosing words that will either help *eliminate* something from your life or help *create* something new in your life."[3]

I will define an affirmation simply as an "I am" statement. Affirmations can be positive or negative. It all depends on what words follow "I am." You use affirmations every day in your mind and in conversation. Most people use it for negative and are completely unaware that they're even using affirmations.

After this chapter, you're going to hear affirmations all over the place: I'm so dumb. I'm such a slacker. I am stressed. I'm such a bad mom. Sometimes we say these things in jest to joke around, and sometimes we don't say them out loud, we say them silently. I'm not good enough. I'm not pretty enough. I'm not smart enough. I am ugly. I am nothing. I am poor. I am lazy. I am procrastinating.

The words I hear people say about themselves can be absolutely shocking. After practicing affirmative language for the past few years, I have become so utterly sensitive to the power of words that I find myself aching inside when people unknowingly cut themselves down, even under the guise of being honest or vulnerable. Words create. If we consistently use negative affirmations, we will continue to create the negative. Even something as seemingly small as regularly declaring, "I am stressed out!" is a surefire way to stay stuck.

When we confront negative feelings, it is important to differentiate between these feelings and our identities. We can be so quick to use "I am" statements to describe our feelings that we risk confusing our feelings with our identity. I have had to correct myself many times to rephrase a statement from "I am" to "I feel." Changing "I *am* stressed out" to "I *feel* stressed out" realigns my sense of self and keeps me in control of my life. I am now enabled to act for myself and not be acted upon. I am not a victim. I may feel a particular feeling, but I am not that feeling, and I retain the power change how I feel.

Changing your language to the positive does not mean that you are ignoring reality. You are simply aiming to create a better reality. Words create. Continue to use negative words and affirmations and you will continue to stay stuck. If you want a change, then you must start talking differently.

Why Affirmations Hold Power

Don't be fooled into thinking affirmations are a hokey feel-good tool. Affirmations hold enormous creative power for two deeply important reasons.

1. It is a set-up statement that instantly creates an image in your mind. If I say, "I am overwhelmed," how does that affect the image of myself in my head? I see a picture of myself being overwhelmed. I see myself not being able to handle the responsibilities and deadlines in my life. If I say, "I am so stupid," I instantly see an image of myself not being able to solve problems and of me failing in my choices. "I am" statements are descriptions of an image (see + say). With both these elements triggered, the way we feel

is an immediate match. Affirmations trigger all three creation elements instantly. Whoa. Yes, indeed. Use with great care.

2. "I am" statements are sacred words. There are many names for God in the scriptures. One of the less commonly spoken names is the name I Am. God told Moses to tell his people that "I Am hath sent me unto you" (Exodus 3:14). I Am is a name of God, and it holds sacred creative power. Whatever words follow "I am" immediately create an image. And what we say influences what we see, and what we see and say influence what we feel. Feelings bring actions and actions bring results. A domino effect has quickly been set in motion for creation.

I am sure you have heard of using affirmations in the positive: I am smart. I am beautiful. I am succeeding. Saying these types of statements when you don't believe them or feel them can feel kind of silly. The number one complaint I hear from people regarding affirmations is "I feel like I'm lying."

When you understand the sacred creative power within an affirmation, you begin to see "I am" statements are not boastful or prideful. They are creative statements. You say them so you can create them. It is the first step, not the last step.

I love to use this tool with my kids. If they are feeling scared about something, I invite them to use affirmations to change their thoughts and feelings: I am safe. I am protected. I am peaceful. I am happy. My kids certainly don't feel that way in the beginning, which is why we use the statements to create something different. The words create new images, which bring new feelings.

If I feel worried or nervous about an upcoming event, I use affirmations to change those feelings. Remember, those negative emotions exist because I have a negative image. Perhaps I have envisioned a worst-case scenario. If I want to change my feelings, I must change what I see and say. Affirmations instantly trigger all three factors in the equation, which is why it is one of my favorite tools for creating.

I have even used affirmations when my alarm goes off early in the morning. *I am tired* may be the initial affirmation that comes to mind. If I allow this affirmation to persist, I will not get up. Instead, even if I do feel tired initially, I change my words and image so I can change my actions. *I am rested. I am getting up. I am excited about my morning routine. I am going to have an amazing day.* You'd be surprised what repeating those affirmations over and over can do even in a warm bed at 5:45 a.m. Affirmations create.

Journal Questions

Think about something in your life right now that is not what you want it to be. Perhaps it is a relationship, goal, or trial. Identify the three creation elements in this experience:

1. What image do you see in your mind when you think of this?
2. What words do you use to describe this situation? How do these words make you feel?
3. Are you ready to turn it around and change what you see and say so you can feel different? Prepare for magic.

CREATING AFFIRMATIONS

Discovering Your Words

Yehuda Berg said, "Words are singularly the most powerful force available to humanity. We can choose to use this force constructively with words of encouragement, or destructively using words of despair. Words have energy and power with the ability to help, to heal, to hinder, to hurt, to harm, to humiliate and to humble."[4]

Affirmations are powerful. So how do you create affirmations specific to your own needs? Select one thing in your life that doesn't feel good. Write down the negative affirmations you have been saying that have created your feelings. This serves as a release tool of writing out the negative thoughts, as well as a framework for creating positive affirmations in the next step.

Negative Affirmations

____

____

____

____

____

Choosing New Words

Look to your list of negative affirmations and write two opposite positive affirmations. Think of "I am" statements, which embody a completely healed situation. Consider using attributes, feelings, actions, and details that lead to the transformation required for you.

Positive Affirmations

____

____

____

____

____

If I am struggling with my body image, I may have the negative affirmation of "I am fat." After I identify my negative affirmation, I can create positive affirmations to counter the negative and create a supportive body image. I love my body. I am grateful for my body. I am taking care of my body. I am healthy. I am fit. I am making healthy food choices. I am excited about exercise. These words create a new powerful image of how I see myself in this area of development.

This exercise is exceptionally revealing to the influence negative affirmations are having upon your experience. Happily, even just the process of writing out new positive affirmations will instantly shift those negative feelings to something much more positive. You may become a believer simply from this step alone.

Imagine what can happen if you read and say your list often! To truly believe something new, you must train your mind with new thoughts and beliefs. It will take time, your mind is very practiced with the old ones. Place your list in a prominent place where you can see it often and say them with conviction every day. Remember, saying it creates it.

Below is a collection of positive affirmations by Louise Hay to help you get started:[5]

- **Affirmations for the Physical Body:** I am pure beauty. My body is a beautiful expression of my individuality. I am a beautiful person. I love and treasure my body. I feel glorious, dynamic energy. I am active and alive. Wellness is the natural state of my body. My body takes me everywhere easily and effortlessly. My mind and body are in perfect balance. I am a harmonious being. I am pain free and totally in sync with life. I am at home in my body. All is well. I am grateful for my healthy body. I love life.
- **Affirmations for Loving Yourself and Others:** I am worthy of love. I am a radiant and joyous person. I am loved beyond comprehension. I am worthy of infinite and unending compassion. Happiness flows freely from me. Love rises from my heart in the face of difficulty. The love within me flows through me in every situation. I feel profound empathy and love for others and their own unique paths. I am authentic, true, and expressive. I have infinite capacity for love and affection. I see my parents as tiny children who need love. I am surrounded by love. Nourishing myself is

a joyful experience. I am worth the time spent on my healing. Love is powerful. Your love and my love. I accept my power. I rejoice in love I encounter every day. I am surrounded by love. All is well. I am comfortable looking in the mirror, saying, "I love you; I really love you." I open my heart and sing the joys of love. I go beyond barriers to possibilities. I love every cell of my body. I deserve the best, and I accept it now. All my needs and desires are met before I even ask. I love myself just the way I am. I am an open channel for creative ideas. I forgive everyone in my past for all perceived wrongs. I release them with love. My heart is open. I speak with loving words. As I forgive myself it becomes easier to forgive others. I look within to find my treasures. I am patient, tolerant, and diplomatic. All is well in my world.

- **Affirmations for Life Trials:** I have the ability to overcome any challenge life gives me. I carry strength and resilience with me. I honor my own life path. Success is defined by my willingness to keep going. I receive grace. Life supports me in every possible way. All that I need to know at any given moment is revealed to me. I handle my own life with joy and ease. I now choose to release all hurt and resentment. I am safe.
- **Affirmations for Finances:** I am unlimited in my wealth. All areas of my life are abundant and fulfilling. Abundance flows freely through me. My intuition is always on my side. My income is constantly increasing.
- **Affirmations to Create Your Day:** Today is going to be a really really good day. Today is the future I created yesterday. Today I create a wonderful new day and a wonderful new future. Every experience I have is perfect for my growth. Every decision I make is the right one for me. I choose to feel good about myself each day. Everything in my life works now and forevermore. My life is joyously balanced with work and play. All that I seek is already within me. My day begins and ends with gratitude and joy.

Empowerment Tool #2: Mantra Meditation

Loving yourself is the foundation of everything in your life. If you have sincere love for yourself, speak with kindness, and exercise compassion, grace, and quick forgiveness, I promise that your entire life will dramatically transform. Why? Because when you love yourself, you make different choices. When you love yourself and quickly receive grace, you are empowered to do the same for others. This is such an incredibly beautiful place to live your life from.

Getting to this place, and maintaining this place, requires consistent effort. It requires clearing tools to get rid of the false identity, and it requires empowerment tools that empower the true identity.

MANTRA MEDITATION

The second empowerment tool is mantra meditation. Ma Jaya Sati Bhagavati stated, "Quiet the mind, and the soul will speak."[6] If you don't have experience with meditation, let me assure you that this particular meditation is quick and easy. Mantra meditation is meditating upon a single word or phrase that you repeat over and over again in your mind. This is similar to an affirmation, only experienced from a place of quiet stillness.

Here is the mantra I want you to repeat to yourself: "I love and accept you, [state your name.]" It's important to say your name. Here's how to put it into practice:

1. Sit comfortably with a straight back in a quiet place.
2. Close your eyes, put your hands over your heart or rest them comfortably palms up in your lap.
3. Begin with three deep inhales and exhales through the nose to relax your body and center your mind.
4. Repeat the mantra out loud or silently in your mind on each slow inhale and exhale for five minutes.

That's it! You're done!

Five minutes is not long. Though if you've never done something like this before, it may feel that way at first. You can set a timer on your phone or download a meditation app that will do an easy countdown for you. Truthfully, even one minute is better than nothing, though I personally love what happens when extending it to five. It seems to be the perfect amount of time to move past the stage of using the mantra like a tool and to transition into a place where I actually feel the mantra taking effect inside of me. This meditation is powerful, especially over time.

At the time of this writing, I have done this meditation nearly every day for more than a year. Never more than five minutes, some days for only one. Because this is part of my daily practice, I often find myself pulling this mantra out at all times of day. I am a different person today than the person of a year ago because of this mantra.

Other than breathing, it is the absolute fastest way I have found to immediately connect to my true self.

There are many other uses for this mantra. I use this mantra throughout my day in the following scenarios, and, instantly, my feelings of being less vanish! It's a magic mantra! It's powerful and fast! If you practice this mantra regularly, you will find that you automatically repeat it in your mind throughout the day when you need it.

When you have thoughts of comparison? State the mantra. When someone disappoints you? State the mantra. When someone says something mean? State the mantra. When someone makes you feel like a failure? When you feel embarrassed? When you feel angry? When you feel overwhelmed and totally stressed out? When you're scared and afraid? When you feel like you're not enough? State the mantra.

You can more or less apply this mantra to any setting in your life and it will always help. Our negative emotions are most often rooted in the need to feel love and belonging, which is why this works even in situations that seem unrelated. It all comes back to love as your foundation.

Is it any wonder that Jesus taught love as the greatest commandment and promised that all else would fall into place if we followed this principle first? It is an eternal truth. It never fails. Ever. Love requires consistent work and effort. Just like a seed, it must be cared for and nurtured. If you will dedicate even a few minutes a day, I promise you this is enough to change your life. How could five minutes truly change your life? It's all about the compound effect.

The Compound Effect

In his book *The Compound Effect*, Darren Hardy says:

> The Compound Effect is the principle of reaping huge rewards from a series of small, smart choices. What's most interesting about this process to me is that, even though the results are massive, the steps, in the moment, don't *feel* significant. Whether you're using this strategy for improving your health, relationships, finances, or anything else for that matter, the changes are so subtle, they're almost imperceptible. These small changes offer little or no immediate result, no big win, no obvious I-told-you-so payoff. So why bother?
>
> Most people get tripped up by the simplicity of the Compound Effect. . . .
>
> What they don't realize is that these small, seemingly insignificant steps completed consistently over time will create a radical difference.[7]

So let's look at a fascinating example of the compound effect in action. Darren describes it using the story of the magic penny:

> If you were given a choice between taking $3 million in cash this very instant and a single penny that doubles in value every day for 31 days, which would you choose? . . .
>
> Let's say you take the cold hard cash and your friend goes the penny route. On Day Five, your friend has sixteen cents. You, however, $3 million. On Day Ten, it's $5.12 versus your big bucks. . . .
>
> After 20 full days, with only 11 days left, [your friend] has only $5,243. How is she feeling about herself at this point? . . . Then the invisible magic of the Compound Effect starts to become visible. The small mathematical growth improvement each day makes the compounded penny worth $10,737,418.24 on Day Thirty-one, more than three times your $3 million. . . .
>
> Very few things are as impressive as the "magic" of compounding pennies. Amazingly, this "force" is equally powerful in every area of your life.

The clearing tools and empowerment tools that I have introduced in this book are magic pennies. Let's refresh our memories by listing these tools.

Clearing Tools

1. Little Black Notebook
2. Write and Burn
3. Look Somewhere New
4. Get Grounded in Nature
5. Become the Observer
6. Deep Breathing
7. Move Your Body
8. Emotional Freedom Technique
9. Forgiveness
10. The Redeeming and Enabling Power of Jesus Christ
11. Call upon God and Command Satan to Depart

Empowerment Tools

1. Affirmations
2. Mantra Meditation
3. Grace (found in chapter 7)
4. Nurturing Rituals (found in chapter 7)
5. The Artist Date (found in chapter 7)
6. Social Media Boundaries (found in chapter 8)
7. Surround Yourself with Good Influence (found in chapter 8)
8. Vision Journal (found in chapter 9)
9. See Freedom (found in chapter 9)
10. Fast Forgiveness (found in chapter 11)

These tools are all small and simple, don't take much time, and may seem insignificant in the moment. But if you consistently spend even a few minutes a day with a favorite tool, after thirty-one days, you will see an amazing difference in your life. Press onward for two, three, four, five, six months, and the compound effect will become even more dramatic.

When I told you that I looked back on the last year of doing a single five-minute meditation and how it has completely changed me, you can see how this change could happen. I want this to happen for you too! I invite you to commit to your choice of a clearing tool and an empowerment tool for at least thirty-one days. Choose to believe in the power they hold. After all, "by small and simple things are great things brought to pass" (Alma 37:6).

Life in your true identity is peaceful, calm, and full of light, hope, and love. You were designed to live life from this place. These tools will help you do just that. They help you put off the false identity and live in your true identity. You can do this! As you do, you will shine and give others permission to do the same. This is the true you.

Notes

1. *Merriam-Webster's Collegiate Dictionary*, s.v. "as (*adv.*)," accessed April 28, 2018, http://www.merriam-webster.com/dictionary/as.
2. *American Dictionary of the English Language* (1828), s.v. "hang."
3. Louise Hay, "The Power of Affirmations," *Louise Hay*, n.d., https://www.louisehay.com/the-power-of-affirmations/.
4. Yehuda Berg, "The Power of Words," *HuffPost*, updated Nov. 17, 2011, https://www.huffingtonpost.com/yehuda-berg/the-power-of-words_1_b_716183.html.
5. See "Daily Positive Affirmation from Louise Hay," *Louise Hay*, https://www.louisehay.com/affirmations.
6. "Ma Jaya Sati Bhagavati Quotes" Goodreads, https://www.goodreads.com/quotes/502743-quiet-the-mind-and-the-soul-will-speak.
7. Darren Hardy, *The Compound Effect: Multiplying Your Success, One Step at a Time* (New York: Vanguard Press, 2010), 9–10.
8. Darren Hardy, *The Compound Effect: Jumpstart Your Income, Your Life, Your Success* (New York: Vanguard Press, 2011), 10–11.

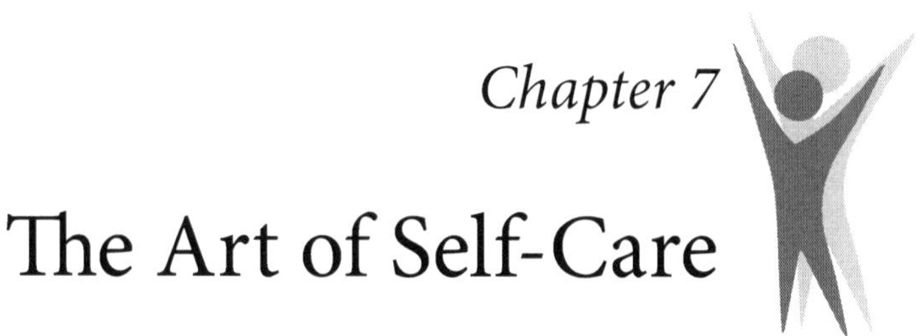

Chapter 7
The Art of Self-Care

On my wedding day in 2007, my wise father passed the torch to my husband, Ben, with this bit of marital advice: "Make sure you feed her and put her to sleep on time. If you can do those two things, it'll all work out!"

Coming from a man who had lived with me for over two decades, you could say he was quite familiar with both my false identity and my true identity. He had observed some important elements that kept my false identity at bay and made me more pleasant to be around. Needless to say, my husband has relied on this advice countless times and, happily, it works just like my dad promised him it would.

Now, food and sleep may be basic survival strategies that cure an emotional meltdown or bring hope back into view, but just imagine what can happen when self-care is allowed to rise above the level of surviving and enter into the realm of thriving.

We have all experienced the false identity emerge when we neglect our own self-care. Did you pull an all-nighter? Did you eat junk all week? Did you spend every waking moment only responding to others' needs? Have you showered and gotten fully dressed? Did you move your body or did you disconnect with a screen instead? When did you last spend time in nature? When you neglect your own self-care to any degree, living in your true identity is far more difficult. Your true identity must be nurtured and fed with daily consistency.

ARE YOU MOVING AWAY FROM PAIN OR TOWARD JOY?

Most people will care for themselves only far enough to no longer feel pain physically, emotionally, mentally, or spiritually.

Consider the scale in the image below. The further away you get from pain, the better you feel. If being at a six crosses over to the joy side, then not feeling pain can seem good enough. Content, many people stop or minimally maintain the self-care efforts here and easily sink back to the pain side of the scale in life's natural ebb and flow. It can feel like a never-ending cycle of always trying to get away from pain, instead of eagerly seeking to keep moving toward joy. Where do you fall on the scale?

When you choose to keep moving toward joy, you embrace nurturing rituals and the art of self-care. Here, you spend your time in the eight-to-ten range of joy. Life brings a natural fluctuation, similar to the waxing and waning of the moon. At times, we are increasing in light, and other times we are decreasing, but you don't have to go through the entire spectrum. Living in balance allows you to subtly shift up and down, but you are anchored by your nurturing habits.

Because your true identity is joyful, this range is a beautiful place where your true identity easily shines through. It is a lifestyle to live here. This lifestyle is built upon nurturing rituals, which we will explore in a moment.

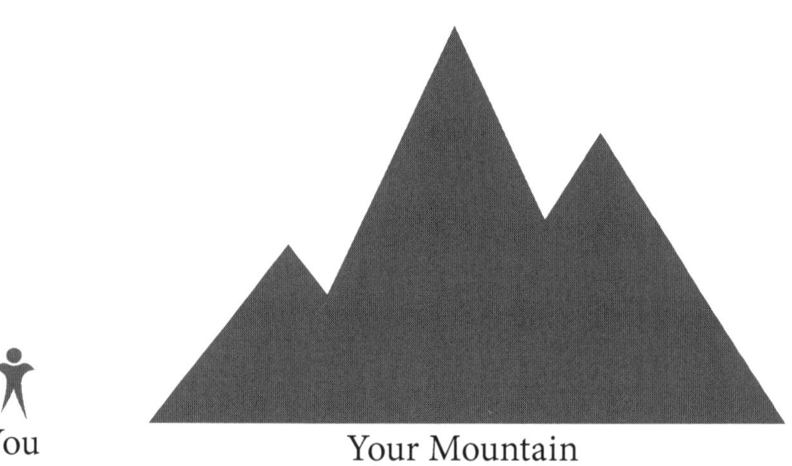

RESPONSIBILITIES, STEWARDSHIPS, COMMITMENTS, CHALLENGES, TRIALS, AND RELATIONSHIPS

So how does this eight-to-ten range of joy correspond to your environment? How is it affected by trials, challenges, and setbacks? Looking at the image above, can you remember a time when your life felt totally overwhelming? When every day was an uphill battle? How well did you care for yourself during this time? Were you nurturing yourself with love and grace every day? I didn't think so.

When you are not giving yourself the love, care, and nourishment that you need, you stay small and your mountain grows tall. If you are living at a level two and experience a level three problem, it's bigger than you are. You can try to conquer your mountain little by little, but, still, you will inevitably feel exhausted and discouraged. There is a much easier way to climb this mountain. It involves changing the scale of the drawing.

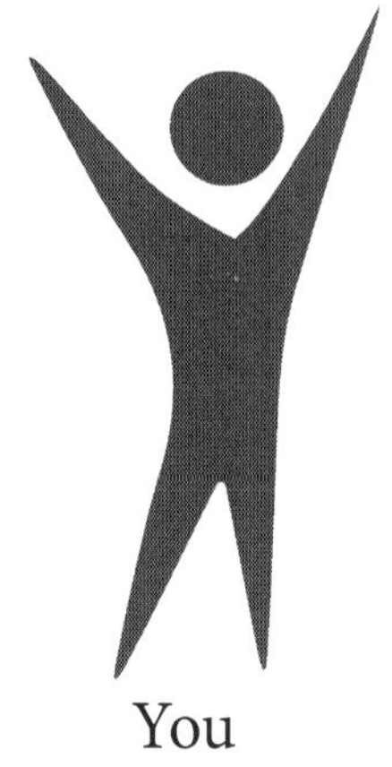

Practicing the art of self-care makes you grow taller. When you grow the image of yourself, when you nourish yourself, you figuratively grow taller and become bigger than your mountain. You become bigger than your trials and challenges. You become bigger than the stress and feelings of overwhelmingness. If a level three problem comes along and you're at a level nine, you can easily handle it.

What is your own pattern? When your schedule seems overwhelming, when the needs of others press upon you, when trials show up in your life and your mountain starts to feel oh so big, do you amp up your self-care and grow taller to conquer it? Or do you put your self-care to the bottom of the list in an effort to fight fires and tackle what is immediately in front of you? Do you grow big or do you unintentionally become smaller and smaller?

If you can learn to gracefully nourish yourself every day, it will provide the growth you need to be taller than your mountain. Life will always have opposition, and you will always have commitments and responsibilities and challenges. However, the scale of those challenges is directly related to the scale of your own self-image. If you're tall, most challenges feel small.

If you're small, most challenges feel tall.

With consistent self-care, you'll also find many of your self-imposed challenges slip away because you are making better choices that nurture you. Life is so much easier and more beautiful when you are well cared for. The view is amazing! You see above the mountain. Your capacity to help serve others and fulfill your own personal mission is greatly enhanced.

If it's so great to be well cared for, why do we neglect ourselves? I have heard every excuse and used them all myself. For years. Why do we *not* do it? Because we don't believe we can. Our false identities tell us that caring for ourselves is selfish. That we don't have the time. That we don't have the money. That we don't have the necessary help. That we don't have support. That we don't have the health. That we don't deserve it. It all boils down to belief, and, by now, you should be able to recognize all of those negative affirmations as statements of the false identity. Just writing those phrases out makes me feel all closed up. It is only impossible if you believe it to be so.

RESOLVING RESISTANCE

Do you believe that you can obtain the amount of self-care that you need to thrive? If you have any resistance to upping your self-care, ask yourself why? What belief is holding you back? On what level do you believe it? Spiritually, mentally, emotionally, or physically? Hopefully this book has helped you believe you need self-care on a mental level. Do you believe it yet on an emotional and physical level? What clearing tools can you use to let go of this belief? What empowerment tools can you use to believe something new and supportive? What logistics are holding you back?

Logistics have always been my favorite excuse. I can't because I have small children and I'm the only one that can watch them. I can't because no one will cover for me. While different seasons in life will absolutely influence your availability, there is always a way to work things out if you open your mind and think outside the box. What if those logistics were solved?

Last year, a neighboring young mother asked if I would be interested in trading childcare for one afternoon a week so we could each attend the temple. I felt like my entire life expanded in that one question. For several months we swapped babysitting for a few hours a week. I was so grateful she thought outside the box. It was a win-win solution.

What creative ideas can you think of to help solve the logistics problem? If you still feel stuck on logistics, this is a great topic to bring up in conversation with your support system of family and friends. Brainstorm together and counsel on ways that you can support each other in receiving the care you both need.

CHANGING HABITS

Ideally, we want to live in a direction moving toward joy, not just moving away from pain. This will require you to take a few extra steps to move past being content with surviving, to live in the realm of truly thriving. It is worth the added effort, and once you spend any significant amount of time in the thriving zone, you never, ever want to go back to just surviving. Better yet, your true identity shines in this zone because you are honoring yourself with love and care. You are more fully living your own portion of the commandment to "love thy neighbor as thyself" (Matthew 22:39).

Truth be told, I have spent many years of my adult life in the survival zone, moving away from pain. I have had an on-again, off-again morning ritual of journaling, prayer, and scripture study, but my tendency to sleep in on weekends and stay up too late made getting up early difficult and inconsistent. I have long struggled to commit to a regular exercise routine, and my serious, focused personality prefers work over play. The only habit I have long sustained with impressive regularity is my diet. I've eaten a clean, non-processed, whole-food diet for the past nine years, and it has been a wonderful steady support to my life. Otherwise, my life is splattered with on-again, off-again bursts of resolve to change my patterns.

Every New Year would come and go, and I would write down the same goals as the year before. Intuitively, I knew these reappearing goals were keystones to upgrading my life: Get up early. Go to bed early. Exercise. Meditate. Do something fun. Play.

My true identity had been trying to send me a message of what will help her shine for many years, but there were long periods when it all seemed too hard. My mountain was far too big. And I was far too small.

Changing habits when you are in the pain zone or survival zone can seem monumental. It's a lifestyle upgrade, and it disrupts the homeostasis of all that is familiar and long practiced. The other challenge with a habit goal is that it lasts forever. Achievement goals have deadlines, and you know when they are done. Habits, though, are a different category entirely. I can last a few days trying something new, but soon the fuzzy forever part of the equation makes me feel like I can work on this later when it becomes more comfortable.

SET A STREAK RECORD

For me, everything changed when I took an online goal-setting course that differentiated habit goals to be time bound. "Set a streak record for your habit goal," my teacher explained. "Pick how many days in a row you want to have a running streak and work for that. Put an X on the calendar each day you do your goal and see how many X's you can get in a row. Try not to break the chain."

Somehow, ninety days of getting up early sounded more manageable than "forever." Every lasting habit change that I have today, started with a streak record. A forty-day meditation challenge turned into three years and counting! Seventy-five days of yoga turned into a daily practice I can't live without. Steadily, I have added habit upon habit to create a framework of self-care that has me living in the thriving zone in the eight-to-ten range of joy. It's taken time and commitment to get here, mixed in with some messiness that naturally comes from upgrading your life. Nonetheless, I never, ever want to return to simply surviving!

Today, my self-care rituals can take up to three hours throughout a day. That may sound like a ton of time. Yet, magically, time is a whole new dimension in the eight-to-ten range of the scale. Life is slower, I have free time, and I'm doing more and have more responsibilities, yet it all feels beautifully slow and manageable. I rarely feel anxiety or stress. I am kinder, more content, more present, and I am rapidly progressing in many areas of personal development. I have time for hobbies, friendships, and one-on-one time with my kids and husband. I read lots of books, spend time outdoors, and have more order in my home. We enjoy home-cooked meals each night and time together as a family, and my house is clean and my laundry is done. I feel so much more capable in loving others because I have learned to love myself. If I stop the self-care, my ability to manage so many different parts of life is quickly reduced and I revert back to the struggle of life happening to me as I scramble to keep up and not collapse in utter defeat.

How is this even possible? How does time shift like that? There are only so many hours in a day, so how is it that I can have greater order in my life when I'm dedicating more time to self-care? Turns out it's science.

THE SCIENCE OF SELF-CARE

I recently watched a video on YouTube called "Amazing Resonance Experiment!"

The experiment begins with an administrator pouring salt onto a vibrating plate. The vibration comes from a tone generator. As the vibration gradually increases, the salt bounces around and then quickly organizes itself into a geometric pattern. In the beginning, the low vibration forms a basic pattern. A circle. With each higher vibration change, there is a period of disruption. The salt dances around in a bit of chaos and then quickly orders itself into a new pattern of greater intricacy. The principle becomes clear: the higher the vibration, the more complex the pattern.[1]

Vibration plays a pivotal role in our daily life. Words have vibration. Thoughts have vibration. Hurtful words are a lower vibration than the high vibration of inspiring words. Activities have vibration. Watching reality TV is a much lower vibration than gardening. Every emotion we feel has a unique vibration level. We intuitively know this when we say things like "She's in a low spirit" or "She's in a high spirit."

So how does this relate to self-care? In the video demonstration, the higher vibration results in a more complex pattern of order. When you live life at a higher vibration, you have order over more things. You're naturally more productive, you experience more patience and love in your relationships, and you solve problems and find solutions more easily. You're bigger than your mountain, and you steward more areas well.

If you live life at a lower vibration, your capacity is far less. You may only be able to manage order in one or two areas. Anything beyond that is too much. Self-Care is the practice that helps you live life at a higher vibration. The higher your vibration, the more order in your life and the more joy you feel.

So how do you maintain a consistently high vibration? Choose high vibration words. Choose high vibration thoughts. Practice high vibration activities. At the risk of repeating myself again, what you see, say, and feel directly influences your vibration. You must consciously create your life so that it is moving toward joy, or you'll settle into a life of survival.

Change is not always a smooth process. From this same experiment, you can see the patterns of salt slightly fall apart each time the vibration is raised before order ensues once again. Any change we experience in life causes some momentary disruption. Don't be surprised when you attempt to upgrade your habits and things feel momentarily chaotic and unfamiliar. This is natural. Press forward until you settle into your new intricate pattern.

THE ART OF SELF-CARE

Self-care is an art form. It is developed over time, and you gradually get better with practice as you learn what habits and rituals serve you best. You will become more aware of the vibration of certain activities.

Taking a break to browse social media is a lower vibration than taking a break to go for a walk outside—which is typically a high vibration. With practice, you will make better choices for yourself and find yourself moving toward joy and not just moving away from pain.

We'll study the art of self-care in three areas: the art of grace, the art of ritual, and the art of delight.

THE ART OF GRACE

Seed of Grace

by Brooke Snow

Daily the farmer works and toils
He sows his seeds in nurtured soil
Clears the ground of noxious weeds
All for hope in harvesting
By and by the seeds grow strong
With abundance in their song
His efforts have paid off again
But can he claim the glory when
The sun shone high for many days
The rain did visit when he prayed
The seeds attained their pure design
And bounty gives in more supply?
The grace of God is freely given
The rain and sun sent from heaven
But only those who plant their seeds
Will reap the fruit of what can be

The first time I really understood the balance between works and grace was when I read *A Marvelous Work and a Wonder*, by LeGrand Richards. He explains grace in the metaphor of a farmer. The farmer plants his seed, prepares the ground, weeds, but still cannot claim credit for the growth or harvest of his crop. For who sent the rain? Who allowed the sun to shine? Who created the seeds that fulfill their design to grow? It is God that brings the rain, God that brings the Sun, God that helps things grow. These are the elements of God's grace.[2]

Yet there is a difference between the seed that is never planted and the one that is carefully placed in soil. The rain falls and sun shines on every person, but only those who do the work to plant themselves in the ground will receive grace to transform into who God created them to be.

We all have the seed of divinity within us. We were each created for a divine purpose with a unique and wonderful mission to fulfill. But we do not realize this potential unless we consistently plant ourselves in the ground to receive His enabling and redeeming power. There are things we must do. Our efforts are small in comparison. Nevertheless, these small efforts reap great rewards. The prophet Alma taught, "By small and simple things are great things brought to pass" (Alma 37:6).

Self-care is the practice of daily placing yourself in the ground to receive the grace of God. You show up in a position to receive and grow. God then transforms you through His grace. He grows you taller than your mountain, leads you to marvelous places, and equips you to accomplish marvelous things. But you have to show up. You have to plant yourself in the ground in order to grow.

Empowerment Tool #3: Grace

There are many disciplines that plant you in the ground to receive grace: prayer, meditation, scripture study, repentance, and forgiveness, to name a few. Any practice that aligns your body/mind/spirit to God will place you in the ground ready to receive His grace for your own ongoing transformation. Making this a daily practice is when the real magic starts to happen. Consistency is key. Mastering the act of simply showing up every day is made easier when it becomes a ritual.

THE ART OF RITUAL

Empowerment Tool #4: Nurturing Rituals

The evening and the morning routines in your life are the most important moments of your day. How you start and how you finish stand as bookends to all that occurs in between. You have more control over these sacred hours than any other time, as other people and events largely influence everything that happens in the middle. If you can learn to create a special routine in the morning and evening with great meaning to you, it will change your life.

As a missionary, I read a talk by Elder Jeffrey R. Holland. He boldly cautioned missionaries by saying, "You make or break your mission every morning of your life. You tell me how those morning hours go from 6:30 a.m. until you are on the street in your mission, whatever time it is; you tell me how those hours go, and I will tell you how your day will go."[3] According to the missionary schedule, these early hours are personal. It is not the time of day missionaries are out serving in the community or teaching others the gospel—what many consider the central purpose for serving a mission. Instead, these hours are meant to be used for exercising the body, mind, and spirit. It is your own sacred, personal ritual time to love yourself so you can then more effectively go and love your neighbor. Elder Holland understood the power these hours hold for personal transformation. It is the time a missionary works on her (or his) own soul. Her own faith. Her own testimony. Her own relationship with God. It stands to reason that a missionary who goes forth to serve the remaining hours of the day, filled with power from using this sacred time, will witness miracles and do great good among those she serves. I have found his observation to still hold true in my life today. I make or break my day in those early morning hours.

In the yogic tradition of a daily Sadhana practice, there is one law: Get up, set up, and keep up. Felice Austin expounds this topic in her book *Awake, As in Ancient Days: The Christ-Centered Kundalini Yoga Experience.* She says:

> If you don't set up for the day, if you don't posture yourself, ready to engage the day, how are you going to keep up? And how are you going to have a set up if things are already happening before you even get up? So first you have to get up before things are happening. Then you can set yourself in a posture, attitude, and commitment, ready to engage. Then you have the potential to keep up. If you keep up, you will start having a momentum above Time. And the effective human is timeless above Time. As long as you feel you are just at the whim of Time, you are not at the level of extraordinary human that is your normal potential.[4]

Just like the magic pennies of the compound effect, your self-care rituals compound over time. In the moment, they may seem inconsequential, small, and even simple. But practiced long term, you begin to experience this momentum above time that Felice describes. In addition, you can look back over months or years and find that you have actually grown from a seed into a young tree. You are transforming, and it is magnificent!

Incremental Progress

Building a ritual full of grace must happen in increments to be sustainable. If getting up early or going to bed earlier sounds impossible right now, start by adjusting your schedule in fifteen-minute increments. Every few weeks, increase it again until you ease into your ideal time and add one new practice in at a time.

God teaches us "line upon line, precept upon precept, here a little and there a little" (2 Nephi 28:30). When Jesus was a child, Luke tells us he "grew, and waxed strong in spirit, filled with wisdom: and the grace of God was upon him" (Luke 2:40). "To wax" means to increase. Jesus increased in spirit, wisdom, and grace. Your own self-care rituals will also wax strong over time, gradually raising your vibration and naturally expanding your capacity to do more and have order over more things.

The evening and morning rituals don't have to be long. They need only be consistent. Master first the discipline of showing up every day. Neal A. Maxwell said, "Steady devotion is better than periodic exhaustion."[5] It's the steadiness that makes the difference. Not the rare marathon moment of intense dedication.

What Should You Include in Your Ritual?

Build your rituals upon high vibration activities that align your mind, body, and spirit. Though I've had a decent morning ritual for many years, I only used it to strengthen my mind and spirit. I would pray, journal, and study scripture. While these practices are still fundamental, it wasn't until I began to integrate my body into my ritual that my prayer and study time enhanced tenfold. I began with only three minutes of yoga before my prayer and study and was amazed at the difference in my ability to receive revelation and to have a clear and active mind.

"The spirit and the body are the soul of man" (D&C 88:15). We're taught that when the body and spirit are connected we "receive a fullness of joy" (138:17). Even though death brings an obvious separation of the body and spirit, we can still live our mortal life in a degree of separation from our body. When you intentionally connect the body and spirit in self-care rituals, you also receive a greater fullness of joy.

My current evening and morning rituals include body, mind, and spirit, and I can testify to the increased power from choosing to marry all three. My preference leans toward breath and yoga because it is so easy to do in almost any setting, and it is powerful enough that even a small amount reaps significant gains. It also easily integrates with other practices such as meditation, prayer, and scripture study.

That being said, there are many ways to use the body. Going for a walk, run, bike ride, hike, or dancing can all be sustainable daily rituals that open the body to connect with your spirit for an increase in joy. Please note that I'm not talking specifically about the principle of physical fitness, though many of these activities may be considered in such a way. There is a need we have to connect to our body for spiritual alignment. When your body, mind, and spirit are actively united, your channel for revelation, ability to learn, and capacity to experience joy are infinitely expanded. If you isolate any of them, you are more limited. The most nurturing self-care will occur when you can integrate all three together.

Watch what happens when you go for a walk or run and also use the time to pray, list gratitude, or repeat affirmations. Watch what happens when you pause for several nourishing inhales and exhales before you pray at night. Watch what happens when you dance to inspirational music that holds an empowering message. Watch what happens when you do a few minutes of yoga to increase the openness and breath flowing in your body before you read scriptures. If you find that you resist certain habits like prayer and scripture study or that they feel disconnected and dull, bring the body into the experience, and it will level up the practice immediately.

Rituals built upon activities that integrate the body, mind, and spirit will always serve to provide the deepest level of nurturing and care that you will find. Even when I was fighting for my life in an emergency helicopter, it was the marriage of these three that saved me, as I repeated an inspiring mantra on each inhale and exhale of my body. Even in a moment of extreme limitation, I managed to connect all three. This taught me that if I'm not yet unconscious or dead, it's always possible to do something.

No Routine Is Still Routine

My dear friend Davina Fear is an amazing documentary photographer who photographs families in their normal day-to-day life. She preps for her "Day in the Life" sessions by interviewing the family to find out about their routines and what a typical day looks like for their family, from the moment they wake up until they fall asleep. Often, people respond that they don't have a routine, and she continually points out that everyone has routines. Even the absence of routine is still a routine.

What is your evening routine? For years, I would have said I didn't have one, but just like Davina points out, my missing routine was still a routine. It involved watching TV until I was too tired to stay awake, falling asleep on the couch with my contacts still in my eyes, makeup on my face, clothes still on, house lights on, too exhausted from the day to make it to my bed. It was not purposeful or helpful. Yet it happened more often than I'd like to admit. It was never fun to wake up at 2:00 a.m. with a sore back and to turn off the lights and make my way upstairs in a sleepy stupor to collapse into my real bed.

For me, I had a loving morning ritual long before I ever had an evening one. Perhaps this is because I'm a morning person. Had I been a night owl, I likely would have perfected my nightly ritual first. Now that I have balanced both ends of the day to be nourishing, I have discovered that they each feed the other. Your nightly ritual sets you up for your morning ritual, which sets you up for your day, which sets you up for your evening, and so it goes day in and day out in a glorious chain of beautiful self-care.

Ayurveda Wellness Rituals to Consider

So what finally clicked for me to implement the missing evening routine? I discovered Ayurveda. An ancient five-thousand-year-old practice of wellness that originates in India and is the sister practice to yoga. Ayurveda teaches gentle self-care rituals for optimal health.

One reason for my lack of an intentional evening routine was not knowing what I should do. Nights when I fell asleep in my bed and not the couch, my routine upgraded to washing my face, brushing my teeth, putting on pajamas, saying a fast prayer, and hopping in bed. Could my evening ritual be even more intentional?

Early to Bed, Early to Rise

Ayurveda prescribes an early bedtime and an early awake time. This started to sound familiar to teachings I already knew: "Cease to sleep longer than is needful; retire to thy bed early, that ye may not be weary; arise early, that your bodies and your minds may be invigorated" (D&C 88:124). Ayurveda also details daily habits that cleanse the body of toxins, allowing the body systems and immunity to begin functioning at their optimal state:

Caring For Your Physical Body

- **Tongue Scraping:** Using a stainless steel, U-shaped tongue scraper, scrape your tongue seven to fourteen times every morning and evening. The white film that gathers on your tongue has already been detoxed by your body and needs to be removed. Your toothbrush doesn't remove even a fraction of what a tongue scraper can.
- **Dry Brushing:** Before you shower, use a dry loofah or natural bristle brush all over your body. Your skin naturally detoxes and regenerates. When you dry brush your skin, you exfoliate and sluff off all the dead cells and allow your skin to breathe, have greater health, and stimulate your lymphatic system.
- **Oil Massage:** Before or after you shower, massage your body with a natural oil like coconut oil or sesame oil. Use long sculpting movements on your bones and gentle circular movements on your joints. Use this time to lovingly thank your body for all it does for you.
- **Drink Warm–Hot Water:** Your digestive gut has pores similar to your skin. Just like your skin pores close up with cold water, so does your gut. Warm water opens the pores and allows your body to more fully absorb the nutrients in your food, increases your digestive fire, and feels extra nurturing.
- **Yoga:** The unique qualities of yoga focus on opening your body and attuning your body, mind, and spirit to be one with Divinity.

Ayurveda is much more detailed than these few lifestyle habits. In my exploration of this fascinating ancient practice, I found these small rituals integrated the body, mind, and spirit in ways I had not before considered. I have found greater health, glowing skin, love and acceptance of my body, strong immunity, weight loss, and a gentle ritual that I can easily sustain, with only a few minutes every morning and evening to care for my true identity.

On an ideal day, my morning and evening rituals roughly look like this:

- **Morning:**
  5:45 a.m. scrape tongue and drink eight ounces of hot water
  6:00 a.m. Kundalini yoga
  6:30 a.m. Kundalini yoga meditation
  6:50 a.m. personal meditation (visualization and affirmations)
  7:00 a.m. prayer
  7:10 a.m. scripture study and drink sixteen ounces of hot water
  7:25 a.m. clearing tool
  7:35 a.m. plan my day
  7:45 a.m. get dressed
  8:00 a.m. breakfast with family
- **Evening:**
  9:30 p.m. dry brush
  9:35 p.m. shower
  9:45 p.m. oil massage and affirmations
  9:50 p.m. brush teeth and scrape tongue
  9:55 p.m. yoga and deep breathing
  10:00 p.m. gratitude meditation and prayer

I love my nurturing evening and morning rituals. I crave them. I look forward to them. They are perfect for my interests and season of life and a far cry from my old habit of falling asleep on the couch before doing anything. The compound effect, by this time, is so profound that I can't imagine not doing them. Thriving is so much better than surviving!

Your ideal evening and morning rituals will look different than mine. Yours may be shorter or longer, earlier or later, or include different activities. Have fun in designing the details that alight your own soul.

Seasons of life and family schedules play a large influence but do not have to be a block in obtaining what you need to thrive right now. Not having a nurturing ritual usually comes from not knowing what your ritual should look like and from limiting beliefs that your own circumstances won't make room for what you really need.

In order to create my ideal, I need to detail what I want to happen, as well as communicate my needs to my family for their support. Every time I upgrade my rituals, it has been a bit messy and has triggered trapped emotions and limiting beliefs that were holding me back. Using the clearing tools from chapter 5 has allowed me to let those things go so that I can move forward. Just like the salt dancing in chaos around the vibrating plate, it's important to not give up during that first stage of disruption. The feeling of finally having things settle into order is worth the persistent effort to reach higher. Press forward. Things will settle into a new, beautiful pattern.

What is one nurturing ritual you can add into your routine? Can you add in a minute or two of deep breathing before you pray? Can you add in fifteen minutes of movement into your day? Can you make a ritual out of kitchen dance parties? Design your ritual to feel loving and gentle and fitting for your life and season. Remember, the art of ritual lies in the steadiness. It is the art of showing up and planting yourself in the ground to receive grace. Begin today. Begin where you are, and wax strong in spirit.

THE ART OF DELIGHT

Life can all too easily become routine. Even the rituals that we intentionally create to support our life can turn stale without a bit of spontaneous delight mixed in to keep it fresh. Like the proverb of our grandparents, "All work and no play makes Jack a dull boy." Creating regular moments for play and curiosity are important to the growth of your own spirit and the alighting of your true identity.

Sometimes we allow busy seasons to overrule the very things that bring delight into our life. We become too busy to take a walk, make music, play a game, sing, dance, create, explore, imagine, connect, behold, wonder, or even laugh. Scheduling in moments of recreation allows you to pause and recreate yourself after the tumult of life breaks you down.

Some people are naturally gifted at having fun and taking time to playfully rest from responsibilities to keep the spark of life burning strong. Others have to be a whole lot more intentional about it. Regardless, the art of finding delight every day will keep you young, happy, hopeful, and balanced.

EMPOWERMENT TOOL #5: THE ARTIST DATE

Julia Cameron, in her groundbreaking book *The Artist's Way,* requires her students to set aside one to two hours a week for an artist date, a date by themselves to fill their well of creativity and delight. She urges, "In filling the well, think magic. Think delight. Think fun. Do not think duty. Do not do what you *should* do—spiritual sit-ups like reading a dull but recommended critical text. Do what intrigues you, explore what interests you; think mystery, not mastery."[6] These artist dates are to become a lifetime tool to keep the spark of creativity alive and nurtured.

I have read her book many times. I have always thought artist dates were a good idea in theory, but in practice it seemed far too difficult to maintain. A date to myself once a week? It sounds amazing! My soul longs for this! But the list of limiting beliefs would surface faster than a beach ball under water. I can't. I don't have time. I don't have anyone to watch my kids. Too many people need me. And so, I'd continue with my nurturing morning ritual thinking that should be sufficient. I was taking care of myself; I didn't need to get regular recreation time in addition to that, did I? Without fail, every few months I'd have an emotional breakdown from the daily grind. I'd cry and crave a tiny vacation from life, and then I would muster onward and repeat it all over again.

It wasn't until this past year that I committed to a weekly artist date. I picked Wednesday nights from 7:00 p.m. to 9:00 p.m. and wrote it on the calendar for the entire year. I set an alarm on my phone, cleared it with my husband, and promised myself that I wouldn't be stood up. Interestingly enough, the emotional meltdowns stopped. I felt an increased spark for life and more creativity. Feelings of resentment for not having time to myself left. I was noticeably happier and a whole lot more fun. I laughed and joked more. Taking time to find delight for myself actually allowed me to find delight in other parts of my day and week.

Pick a time: An artist date can be whatever you want it to be. It need only fill the criteria of being delightful. Prioritizing it by putting it on my schedule has been crucial. If I hadn't scheduled it, it would have been too easy too push off, until I reached a breaking point. The alarms on my phone and my husband's are helpful to enforce my commitment.

Choose a default activity: I found early on that it was important for me to have a default activity. If I didn't have anything specific planned for that time, it felt far less important to follow through. I chose the default of going on a walk, so as to always have something to fill that time.

Make a list of options: Most of my dates have been free and low key. Walks, book-club discussions, free time to read a novel, a relaxing bath, a bike ride, a hike, attending the temple, composing music on the piano, visiting a gallery, crafting, or anything else that feels like a pleasurable delight and recreates my soul. It can be helpful to make a list of options of things you enjoy or find curiosity in and want to explore.

You can easily adapt time for delight into your current season. Maybe it is an unplugged walk outside during your lunch break, taking a new class, resurrecting a past hobby, a photo project, a club, a recreational sport, a community project, or a regular meet up with uplifting friends. Taking the time to brainstorm possibilities for regular personal recreation is nurturing to your true identity.

The more you give yourself permission to act upon your own delightful curiosities, the more you develop your divine nature. You have unique interests specific to your mission in life. Learn to follow those curiosities and desires and make it a priority.

Journal Questions

1. Write down what your own ideal routine includes. Have fun in designing the details that alight your own soul.
2. Describe your ideal evening ritual. What time do you begin getting ready for bed? What practices can you integrate to care for your body,

mind, and spirit? What time are you in bed? Are there any logistics that need to be worked out to support this vision? Are there any limiting beliefs or emotions that need to be cleared to support this vision? What supporting affirmation can you say to help create this for you?

3. Describe your ideal morning ritual. What time do you wake up? What practices can you integrate to care for your body, mind, and spirit? Are there any logistics that need to be worked out to support this vision? Are there any limiting beliefs or emotions that need to be cleared to support this vision? What supporting affirmation can you say to help create this for you?
4. Find Delight. Make a list of delight. What activities spark your curiosity and give you a break from normal life? Can you schedule a regular artist date? When and how could you make that happen?

NOTES

1. "Amazing Resonance Experiment!" posted by brusspup, YouTube, accessed Apr. 28, 2018, https://www.youtube.com/watch?v=wvJAgrUBF4w. You can also see the video on my website at http://blog.brookesnow.com/scienceofselfcare, where you can watch the described experiment.
2. LeGrand Richards, *Marvelous Work and a Wonder* (Salt Lake City: Deseret Book, 1976), 266.
3. Jeffrey R. Holland, seminar for new presidents, Jun. 26, 2011.
4. Felice Austin, *Awake, As in Ancient Days: The Christ-Centered Kundalini Yoga Experience* (Madison & West Publishing, 2014), 169.
5. Attributed to Neal A. Maxwell.
6. Julia Cameron, *The Artist's Way: A Spiritual Path to Higher Creativity* (New York: Tarcher Perigee, 2016), 21.

Chapter 8

Living in the World of Social Media and Comparison

It's a love-hate relationship. I don't think I know anyone who doesn't love and hate social media at the same time. Why is this? We love the connection, yet we hate how it makes us feel. How do we live in the world of social media and comparison and manage to hold the false identity at bay?

As I write this chapter, I have just completed an experiment. A few months ago, one of my favorite authors asked for volunteers to participate in a month-long study for his upcoming book on the topic of digital minimalism. For thirty-one days, participants were asked to abstain from social media and any other optional web use. The timing coincided perfectly with writing my manuscript, and the idea of nurturing my focus and creativity in such an extreme way was compelling.

"Optional" was a tempting word that I could have used to redefine his limited instructions. Wasn't it fundamental that I continue growing my online following for my business? I couldn't just disappear for a month, could I? That was not optional! What if people forgot about me? What if I missed out on something important? How was I supposed to stay connected to my family or friends?

Yet, the extremity of the study is what attracted me to it. I threw caution to the wind and went all in. I chose to access my email once a day and to only allow my routine online shopping purchases for groceries and necessities. Otherwise, everything else was classified as "optional" and therefore I opted out.

To begin, I deleted all the social media apps from my phone, as well as any other app that could be a default time waster for me. This included my email app, the Amazon shopping cart app, and any other app that made browsing on my phone an easy pastime.

The first few days were surprisingly hard. My addictive habits were revealed in striking clarity. Moments of waiting in line, moments between activities, moments of boredom, moments I ached to check in on my favorite people, moments I wanted an escape, moments I just wanted to look something up, moments I just needed some diversion, I'd reach for my phone and then remember that everything was gone. I wasn't going to be able to fulfill that craving right now or later.

As time wore on, the detox symptoms wore off, and I began to forget about my phone. My behavior adapted to my new circumstances. Just as I hoped, my focus and creativity skyrocketed. I'd sit for a writing session and sixty to ninety minutes would pass before I'd look at the clock. Without the conditioning of checking my phone every fifteen minutes throughout the day, the impulse had disappeared. and I could actually get some good work done.

I found myself interacting more intentionally with my kids, and, by and large, my life felt far less rushed and distracted. My mind had space to think, ideas would surface in quiet moments of driving or doing housework. I went to bed with a clear and quiet mind, spending my evenings reading a book rather than watching Netflix. I even resurrected some neglected hobbies, like playing the piano and sewing.

Creativity and focus were high on my list of hoped-for results. I expected those traits to blossom. What I didn't expect were all the other benefits I discovered. First, I spent far less money during this experiment, simply from not being exposed to Instagram and blogs. It's harder to realize you're being sold to when the messaging is delivered from real people you admire and follow. Commercials, sidebar ads, and pop-ups were so much easier to recognize as advertising and to push aside. When my favorite influencer posted about the latest item she received that changed her life, you can guarantee I would click on it and seriously deliberate on whether I wanted my life to magically change too.

Second, my confidence increased. Without the daily exposure to an environment that seduced to comparison, I found myself far more content and satisfied with my own life. I have long advocated for curating social media feeds to only follow inspiring people and to unfollow anyone that triggers thoughts of comparison that make you feel less than enough. This tweak alone can dramatically improve your experience. I have practiced this standard relentlessly for many years. To my great surprise, I found that stepping away from my curated and inspirational feed still had a noticeable positive effect upon my identity. Even if you surround yourself with inspiring people who all contribute encouraging content, there is such a thing as too much of a good thing. You can't spend all day observing a crowd of overachievers without measuring your worth at some point. Giving myself the gift of some space allowed me time to reconnect with who I am, without judging myself against the greatness of someone else.

Stepping away for thirty-one days provided clarity I didn't know I was missing. It's like someone cleaned the fish bowl, or better yet, I climbed right out of the bowl itself! As I stand here now from the outside looking in, I see there is so much more the world has to offer on the other side of the glass. My identity isn't influenced by all the other fish, and I don't see myself in a distorted convex reflection from the side of the bowl.

I invite you to seriously consider the impact social media plays upon your own identity. Do you ever feel less than enough while you scroll the feed? Do you ever compare your full-context life with the tiny square snapshot moments of someone else? Do you ever criticize others or yourself in what you see there? Is all the time you spend there really necessary? Or is it optional?

Think of what your life could be like with less media influence. How would it feel to be more present? To enjoy the people in front of you? To feel content with your own life? To live with less anxiety? To nurture buried hobbies or interests? To quiet the voice of comparison that stays on repeat even when the screens turn off? You really can upgrade your life with a few small boundaries. By small things, great things are brought to pass.

Empowerment Tool #6: Social Media Boundaries

Here are my top tips for creating a social media experience that nurtures your true identity:

- **Curate your feed:** Unfollow anyone that triggers feelings that make you feel less than enough and that make you compare your life in unhealthy ways. This is certainly one of those it's-not-you-it's-me relationships. I have unfollowed plenty of remarkable people, solely because I personally struggled to stay strong in my identity when I saw their posts.
- **Delete social media apps from your phone:** It's the greatest way to enforce moderate usage. Limit your use to desktop computers and spend the rest of your time with more presence.
- **Keep phones out of the bedroom:** Far too many people make social media the last thing they see before bed and the first thing they see when they wake up. There is nothing healthy about this. The time before sleep and just after waking up is sacred time. Your mind is even more impressionable in these moments. Not only do you miss the opportunity to receive personal revelation by filling these quiet moments with distraction but also when you fall asleep with negative affirmations of comparison in your mind, they will play on repeat in your unconscious mind all night long, creating limiting beliefs. To wake up and repeat the experience again further affirms the negative and sets the tone for your entire day.
- **Integrate a digital sunset:** Set a time that phones and screens turn off for the day and stick to it, ideally at least one hour before bed.
- **Commit to only posting in your true identity:** Kindness, truth, integrity, empathy, and compassion are traits of your true nature. Refrain from posting or commenting out of anger, frustration, or offense. Even though your true identity is always within you, make sure that the trail you leave on the internet reflects who you really are, not the false identity of a fleeting moment.

- **Opt out:** There will be seasons when staying away is best. Whether it's a time to work on strengthening your identity or your focus, be okay with needing to take extended breaks as necessary. Use your intuition to know what you personally need for your life right now. Pay attention to when your body feels sick, stressed, anxious, tired, depressed, or any time your hormones are causing you to feel lower than normal. These are not the times to get on social media. Your vulnerability in those moments makes you more susceptible to dipping even further into an environment that so easily yields to comparison.

WHO IS ON YOUR TEAM?

Comparison is the root of why we hate social media. Comparison breeds competition. When thoughts of comparison enter your mind, a subtle form of isolation occurs. It's you against someone else. There is no element of teamwork, only a question of who is better. There can only be one winner when life is a competition. Sometimes you win, when you award yourself the upper hand against someone else. And sometimes you lose, when you judge yourself as less than enough.

When we learn to see other people without the labels or measurements that we attach in the comparing mind of the false identity, a new world opens up, revealing that we are all on the same team.

This is a principle that I'm trying consistently to teach my eight-year-old son. Every afternoon, we have a piano lesson. Most musician parents opt out of teaching their own children, since it can be challenging to the relationship. Despite this, I'm committed and I daily wade through his unguarded emotions that he would likely hide from another teacher. Learning a new skill inevitably includes making a lot of mistakes, something he absolutely dreads. One afternoon, after I corrected his rhythm, he immediately collapsed in defeat, overcome with his weakness of not playing it perfectly all on his own.

"Buddy," I said to him encouragingly, "we're a team! You play the song, and I tell you the good things you did and also how to make it better. When you follow my correction, you become a better pianist. We both do our part."

As I looked at him flopped backwards on the piano bench, crying in defeat, I saw a younger version of myself in him. I recalled the many times I had made mistakes, not only on the piano but also in life, and had collapsed with the mindset that my worth was dependent upon my performance. I shouldn't need help. I should be able to do this on my own. But we were not created to do life alone, and we didn't come here already knowing everything. Making mistakes is part of learning. Growth is part of learning. Teamwork is the only way any of us progress in anything. We need each other.

You've probably heard the term "self-taught" before. Several years back, I read an article arguing that there is no such thing as self-taught anything. You aren't a self-taught musician, or photographer, or gardener, or anything else for that matter.

You may not have had formal lessons, but everyone learns from someone else. Maybe through a book, a YouTube video, talking to someone with experience, or lots and lots of research. We don't learn anything by ourselves. Even the simple life lessons that come to us as a form of inspiration still come from God.

If no one is self-taught, it leads me to believe God designed it this way on purpose. As our Heavenly Father, He wants His children to get along. He wants us to help each other, to need each other, and to build a team—a team in which we can both coach as well as participate in our own growth and progress.

If I were to ask you right now who is on your team, who would you say? My team includes family, friends, favorite authors, teachers, podcasters, Jesus, prophets, the Holy Ghost, neighbors, and even my favorite farmer at the market that grows the vegetables that I feed my family. The list is big and far more reaching than I have detailed here.

When I think of everyone as part of my team, it changes how I feel toward others. I have more gratitude, I'm more open to correction, and I see opportunities for me to contribute to others' lives, because if they are on my team, this means I am on their team as well. I can rejoice in their progress and achievements. I can celebrate when another person succeeds instead of feeling like his or her win makes me lose. We are all in this together.

Your true identity sees the world as a team. Your false identity sees the world as a competition. The best indicator I have found for judging whether it is safe for me to be on social media is this simple perspective: In this moment, do I see the world as my team? Can I rejoice in others' successes? Can I graciously allow others to teach me how to grow and improve? If not, walk away, wait to get on social media.

YOUR INNER CIRCLE

Empowerment Tool #7: Surround Yourself with Good Influence

Your environment has a massive influence on how you perceive yourself. By and large, you get to choose who is in your circle of influence. Jim Rohn famously taught, "We become the combined average of the five people we hang around the most."[1]

In today's world, those five people can come from anywhere. The books you read, the shows you watch, the people you follow on social media, the friends you associate with, and beyond. Who are you giving your attention to? Who do you spend the most time with? How do they influence your identity? Do they help you feed the good wolf inside or the bad wolf?

If you find any of your five people to be toxic to your identity, I encourage you to create some appropriate boundaries. Cut ties if possible or limit the time you must spend with them. Choose your circle carefully. If you don't choose, someone else will choose for you.

Surround yourself with people who encourage your growth and development, who impact your life in positive ways. If you want to be successful, hang around successful people. If you want to feel happy, hang around positive people. If you want to grow in a certain area, find a mentor. You can find mentors anywhere: from a book, a class, a podcast, all the way to someone in your own neighborhood. Influence comes from time spent together. Make sure your top five people are the best people for you. Build your team.

Journal Questions

1. Does your typical social media experience feed your false identity or your true identity?
2. What boundaries can you implement to create a better media experience?
3. Do you typically see social media as your team or your competition?
4. Who are the top five people you spend time with? Do they influence you for the better or worse? How?
5. Are there other people who you would like to spend more time with? Who are they?

Note

1. As quoted in Darren Hardy, *The Compound Effect* (New York: Vanguard Press, 2011), 127.

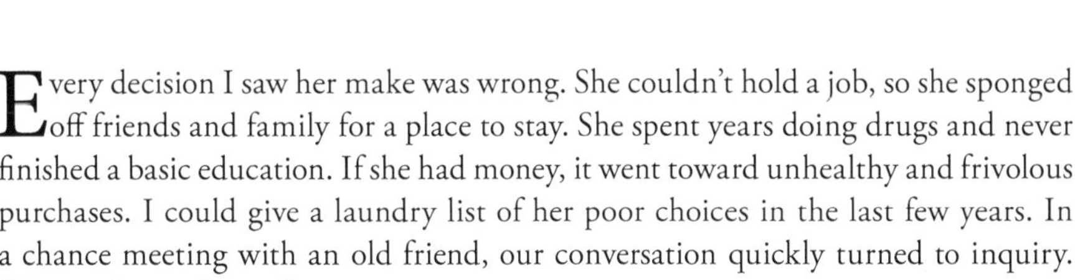

Chapter 9
Seeing the True Identity in Others

Every decision I saw her make was wrong. She couldn't hold a job, so she sponged off friends and family for a place to stay. She spent years doing drugs and never finished a basic education. If she had money, it went toward unhealthy and frivolous purchases. I could give a laundry list of her poor choices in the last few years. In a chance meeting with an old friend, our conversation quickly turned to inquiry. "How is Jenna doing?"

I sighed. The typically frustrated sigh of a family member who is tired and saddened by the choices of someone they love. "She's stuck. Her life is stuck. Nothing she does ever brings her out of her patterns." I went on to detail the latest poor choices in Jenna's life, and we both expressed sorrow to see a life so wasted. The conversation stayed with me on the drive home, my words echoing in my ears, and a growing feeling of guilt washed over me. Nothing I said was intended to create gossip or to hurt Jenna; nonetheless, I regretted my words and felt an eerie sense of contribution to Jenna's choices. *She makes her own choices*, I said defensively in my mind. *You're contributing to the problem*, a voice seemed to say. *Your view of her is just as limiting as her own view of herself.*

A surge of heat flushed my skin as I felt the shame in those words. The very idea that my own image of Jenna could actually be influencing her life. Every limiting and judgmental word I spoke or thought in my mind contributed to the negative energy that already surrounded her daily existence. I could hardly breathe at the very thought of it. *I don't want to do that anymore*, I admitted silently. *I'd rather be a positive influence. But how? How do I learn to sincerely see something better, when the facts are anything but positive?*

Empowerment Tool #8: Vision Journal

I spent the next few days meditating on this question when an idea arose that changed everything—write a journal entry dated in the future describing her life after making positive changes. Immediately I began to write, and watched my image of Jenna transform:

> Jenna is doing amazing. I am so happy to see the empowerment that has come into her life. She loves her new job and is making valuable friendships, acquiring new skills, and everyone gets a delightful taste of her humor. It's so exciting to see how she has come into her own. Working has given her confidence in herself, and she is using her natural gifts and talents that for years went unnoticed but now are flourishing. People love to be around her because she makes them laugh and brightens the mundane routine of life. Best of all, I am so happy to see how her view of herself has changed. She knows who she is and what she is capable of. She is courageous. She knows what it means to fight temptation and win. She is using her past experiences to help other people get back on the right path in their own lives. She is a hero to me and I admire her triumph. I am blessed to know her and have her in my life.

I wrote several pages, moved by the clarity of vision I was creating. The exercise did more than change my feelings toward her—it made me see her differently and love her differently. I saw her potential in the most marvelous way—so powerful, in fact, that I could feel it and, most importantly, I deeply believed it.

I've been taught my whole life about the importance of seeing others the way God sees them. The principle is important. But knowing how to do it has always felt elusive and vague. Until now, I had never experienced such a clear reality of what that may feel like. Many times since, I have used this tool to create a new vision for others and for myself.

How you see others can change their lives. I know this to be true from my own experience. Among the most influential people in my life, all of them have something in common: They see my potential. They believe in me. They see what I can do and become, even when I can't. And, most importantly, they treat me like I have already become that person.

One such person was my college music professor, Dr. Dean Madsen. Every week, I would leave my private lesson with him feeling like I could change the world. Some weeks, I would enter his office in tears and discouragement, yet I would always leave with increased faith and purpose. He consistently expressed the potential he saw in me and described the impact my work would have on the world. Even though I couldn't see those qualities in myself, I leaned on his faith. I trusted him because I knew he loved me. I believed his words, because he believed them. I began to work and act like the person he described. Our ability to see the potential in another truly can change their lives.

It's human nature to see the flaws, to define people by their choices. When it is our family member, child, spouse, parent, or close friend, it is all the more important to truly form a clear picture of the potential they carry within, as our interactions with them are remarkably influential. People know when we don't believe in them. And just as powerfully, they know when we do.

C. S. Lewis carries this vision even further in his book *The Weight of Glory*, saying:

> It is a serious thing to live in a society of possible gods and goddesses, to remember that the dullest and most uninteresting person you can talk to may one day be a creature which, if you saw it now, you would be strongly tempted to worship, or else a horror and a corruption such as you now meet, if at all, only in a nightmare. All day long we are, in some degree, helping each other to one or other of these destinations. It is in the light of these overwhelming possibilities, it is with the awe and the circumspection proper to them, that we should conduct all our dealings with one another, all friendships, all loves, all play, all politics. There are no *ordinary* people. You have never talked to a mere mortal. Nations, cultures, arts, civilizations—these are mortal, and their life is to ours as the life of a gnat. But it is immortals whom we joke with, work with, marry, snub, and exploit—immortal horrors or everlasting splendours. . . . Next to the Blessed Sacrament itself, your neighbour is the holiest object presented to your senses.[1]

There are no ordinary people. The worth of souls is great in the sight of God, with each person holding equal potential to become a god or goddess in His kingdom. Surely, God sees us differently than we see ourselves and differently than we often see one another.

Empowerment Tool #9: See Freedom

So how does one see the way God sees? Must I create a vision journal entry for every person I stumble upon? What about the person who cuts me off in traffic? The irritable neighbor across the street? The politician whose words and actions appear thoughtless or self-serving? The girl on social media whose life seems perfect and untouchable? The friend or family member whose love and approval I can never seem to win? How do I see each person with such potential and love when what I feel is the opposite?

I must see them in their freedom. Free from fear. Free from anxiety. Free from addiction. Free from bad choices. Free from anger. Free from childhood trauma. Free from selfishness. Free from boasting. Free from disease. Free from a closed mind. Free from a closed heart. Free from worry. Free from limited beliefs. Free from abuse. Free from depression. Free from delusion. Free from disability. Free from betrayal. Free from sin. Free from pain. Free from suffering. In this freedom lies the truth. The truth of who you are, the truth of who she is, the truth of who he is.

What does that freedom look like? Can you see how she (or he) looks when you free her from all that holds her true identity back? There was a moment long ago when she was free of everything. In the delightful gaze and wonder as a new infant, she entered this world free. Is she not the same person? Are we not created eternally?

The purpose of this life is to learn and gain experience. Our experiences do not define who we are or what we are worth. They are only opportunities for growth.

Just like the acorn, we always hold the potential inside to grow into a mighty oak. The seed may be sitting atop the ground, and perhaps roughed with dirt, but we nevertheless still hold everything inside to become a mighty tree. Always, the potential is there. It is who we are.

To see one another in freedom is to see the way God sees. The very act of the Atonement of Jesus Christ was an act of freedom:

> And he shall go forth, suffering pains and afflictions and temptations of every kind; and this that the word might be fulfilled which saith he will take upon him the pains and the sicknesses of his people.
>
> And he will take upon him death, that he may loose the bands of death which bind his people; and he will take upon him their infirmities, that his bowels may be filled with mercy, according to the flesh, that he may know according to the flesh how to succor his people according to their infirmities.
>
> Now the Spirit knoweth all things; nevertheless the Son of God suffereth according to the flesh that he might take upon him the sins of his people, that he might blot out their transgressions according to the power of his deliverance. (Alma 7:11–13)

Jesus Christ took upon him every sin, pain, sickness, and infirmity for you and for me so we could be free. Surely, He saw us in our freedom. Surely, this vision of who we really truly are—free from all that binds us in this life—moved Him to fulfill His divine sacrifice.

"Greater love hath no man than this, that a man lay down his life for his friends" (John 15:13). Whom do you see as a true friend in your life? Indeed, someone who loves you, and sees the freedom in you. Jesus continues saying, "Ye are my friends" (vs. 14).

We become free once more when we claim the Atonement for ourselves, just as the apostle Paul decreed, "Stand fast therefore in the liberty wherewith Christ hath made us free, and be not entangled again with the yoke of bondage" (Galatians 5:1). Free yourself from this bondage, free others from this bondage. See the freedom within.

Note

1. C. S. Lewis, *The Weight of Glory* (New York: HarperOne, 1980), 45–46.

Chapter 10

Unity: Next Level Identity

"Is there really that much of a difference between 95 percent and 100 percent?" I asked my husband. It was the summer of 2017 and the continental United States was about to receive a total solar eclipse from coast to coast, a celestial phenomenon that had not occurred for ninety-nine years. Our hometown was projected to witness a 95 percent totality of the event. Ben was arguing for traveling two and a half hours by car to witness the eclipse at 100 percent totality, but I was resisting.

Months earlier the cities in the path of totality had issued emergency preparedness warnings to all residents to gather up food and fuel supplies to last at least two weeks in anticipation of an inpouring of millions of people seeking to view the extraordinary moment. I imagined bumper-to-bumper traffic and other resulting chaos and immediately felt content to stay home. "A 95 percent totality is practically 100," I urged. "Let's stay here."

Ben wasn't convinced. A week went by and he presented the idea again, only this time with a top-secret travel route that included an hour's drive on a dirt road, bypassing all major cities and landing us in the unincorporated town of Bone, Idaho, population two. "I am sure we'd avoid the traffic and we'd still get in the path of totality," he said grinning, happy with his grand compromise. I sighed in agreement.

On August 21, 2017, we awoke early and set out on our adventure. The dirt road slowed our travel to less than thirty-five miles per hour to carefully avoid bumps and holes and most importantly, one of many Black Angus cows whose grazing territory we were trespassing upon. A billowing cloud of dirt trailed behind our van as we bounced onward through the winding hills and sagebrush.

When the dirt road spit us out onto the paved highway cutting through Bone, Idaho, we noticed the population had increased far beyond two. We weren't the only ones who had picked the obscure dot on the map, just among the brave few who navigated through unchartered territory to get there. Nonetheless, we drove a mile or so up the road and pulled off to the side to claim our own spot.

Miles and miles of wide-open space could be seen in every direction. It truly felt like the middle of nowhere, yet the energy and excitement of fellow seekers setting up camp around us added to the anticipation. We donned our special eclipse s and watched the slow travel of the moon passing between the earth and sun to reach a perfect and rare alignment. There really was nothing extraordinary to be seen unless you gazed through the dark protective lenses to reveal the waxing shadow. Once you took the glasses off, it seemed like all was natural in the world, and it was a typical Monday morning.

Until it wasn't. The air suddenly dropped in temperature, the world grew dark, and stars appeared, casting an esoteric glow that seemed unfitting for 11:00 a.m. A breeze picked up, and seconds before totality struck, a hawk soared in a crazed swoop right above my head calling out in declaration of the supernatural.

For ninety unforgettable seconds, we lived in an alternate dimension of time and space. Words could not describe this moment. The air was thick with a metaphysical energy, and we gasped in absolute awe and wonder, gazing at a dark moon with a ring of fire blazing its edges. And then it was over. No one spoke for several moments, almost too shaken by what we had just experienced. There was absolutely a difference between 95 percent and 100 percent.

Pulitzer Prize winner Annie Dillard describes her experience seeing a total solar eclipse with these words: "I had seen a partial eclipse in 1970. A partial eclipse is very interesting. It bears almost no relation to a total eclipse. Seeing a partial eclipse bears the same relation to seeing a total eclipse as kissing a man does to marrying him, or as flying in an airplane does to falling out of an airplane. Although the one experience precedes the other, it in no way prepares you for it."[1]

Totality is infinitely more fantastic. There is an energizing power that comes from the perfect unison of the cosmos. While a partial eclipse is interesting, a total eclipse is an entirely new level.

NEXT LEVEL IDENTITY

Identity has many levels. To begin, we must learn the difference between the false identity and our true identity and nurture our divine nature within. Similar to a total eclipse, the next level comes when we move into total alignment with the Son of God. Just like the moon, we are in our own orbit of flux and progression, at times facing the sun and at times turned away, we wax and we wane. The light we shine to the world is only a reflection from the Son. We shine greatest when we fully face the Son to reflect His light.

In His intercessory prayer in Gethsemane, Jesus models this alignment and reflection of God's glory as He lifts his eyes to heaven saying, "Father, the hour is come; glorify thy Son, that thy Son also may glorify thee. . . . I have glorified thee on the earth. . . . And now, O Father, glorify thou me with thine own self with the glory which I had with thee before the world was" (John 17:1, 4–5). Jesus is fully facing God the Father in total unity, and then he prays that we may do the same. "Holy Father, keep through thine own name those whom thou hast given me, that they may be one, as we are" (John 17:11).

To reach our greatest potential, we must be in alignment. We must be one with the Son.

This concept of oneness with the Divine consistently appears in the practice of yoga, meditation, Buddhism, and many other traditions. It holds transcendent power, the power to transcend the natural man's false identity and fully shine in one's true identity. It is the only way to shine.

When you are one, you have complete unity and alignment with the Divine. You desire the same things, you see the world through the same lens, your thoughts are in alignment, your actions are in alignment, your life is in alignment. It is a beautiful state of unity and pure love. There is no separation between you and the Divine.

How can you tell if you are one with God? If you are one, you feel it. You feel pure love for yourself, for your neighbor, and for God. There is no separation. When you pray, there is no barrier between you and the Lord. It does not feel like you are sending off your prayers to a faraway place, hoping He hears you. You know He loves you, and you feel comfortable in His presence, for you must be in His presence to reflect light. The more you turn toward the Son, the more light you shine.

DEGREES OF SEPARATION AND CONNECTION

CONNECTION TO GOD

SEPARATION FROM GOD

Most people feel a degree of separation from God. The graphic above depicts the degree of separation we feel from God according to how true our view is of ourself and Him. The more truth that exists in how we see ourself and how we see the character of God, the closer our connection to Him. The more false our view of ourself and of God, the greater our separation. Think back on any time in your life that you have struggled with your identity. Ask yourself, what was my relationship with God like at this time? Was I separated in any degree from Him?

When you feel separation from God, you most certainly feel separation in yourself. The two are intricately connected. The false identity separates you from God and separates you from other people. It survives on separateness. Your true identity is naturally connected to God and humanity. The labels and barriers disappear, and you see humanity as your own brothers and sisters. Why? You feel safe. You feel peace, power, capacity, influence, inspiration, vision, courage, fortitude, love, light, and joy in this space. You are empowered from connection. You stop craving the praise and recognition of other people to validate who you are, because you no longer feed off separateness.

When you take down all the walls of separation, you open yourself up to feeling and experiencing everything on a higher level because the limitations are now gone. Separation is a box. It is just another form of limits and unnecessary boundaries that stifle your experience into being less than it could be.

Fear of the False Identity

There's a fear that can exist before the walls of separation come down. It's the dying threat to the false identity. The fear that your separateness is actually what makes you special, that you can only feel important and special if you're separated somehow. The fear that being one with God or being one with your fellow humans will cause you to blend in and lose your individuality. If you have that sneaking fear, let me assure you, nothing could be further from the truth.

Oneness does not mean sameness. If God wanted us to all be exactly the same, He would have made us that way. Instead, He created an infinite variety in everything. You can be one and still be unique and individual. This is a marvelous dichotomy. In fact, when you are in this place of oneness, you will learn more about your uniqueness than you ever could have in the box of separateness. The walls are down, and you can finally see.

OPENING THE DOOR TO UNITY

Each of us waxes and wanes in our unity with God because of opposition from the false identity. At times, fear may prevent us from even desiring unity at all. Such was the case with me. I grew up in the LDS Church and have always been an outwardly faithful Christian. Yet if I were to put myself on the spectrum of connection to God, I would say that I danced the border between seeing a true and false image of myself and God.

Prayer often felt disconnected to me, like I was addressing a letter requiring overnight delivery somewhere very far away. Sometimes, I sent those letters out of obligation and hoped He wouldn't notice the sloppy writing and repetitive message. Other times, I sent no letters at all. Sometimes, I shamefully hoped He wouldn't notice all the details I omitted regarding what went on that day. And yet, scattered here and there were moments I would get a letter back. Moments I felt inspired. Moments I would catch a flash of understanding in who He was and who I was. By and large though, I kept what I considered a respectable distance. That is, until my world fell apart.

I had a mental breakdown and reached a place of great despair. I was suffering from anxiety, PTSD, panic attacks, and depression. I felt overwhelmed and stressed and very far away from everyone in my life, let alone God. I knew what it was like to be gasping for breath physically and need intervention. Now, two years later, I found myself unable to breathe mentally and spiritually. I needed saving of a different kind. I knew that I needed to put my health and wellness in top priority or I would not survive. In my desperation, I gave myself permission to drop everything and focus solely on recovery.

I put my business on hold indefinitely and reduced my commitments. I signed up for a yoga class. I signed up for a meditation class. I started seeing a mentor. I started taking a natural anti-anxiety supplement. And I began practicing more clearing and empowerment tools.

My first breakthrough came when my mentor pointed out that I had a limiting belief about God and invited me to do a write and burn exercise on the topic of "Fear of God." Writing out my feelings revealed to me the degree of separation that I had been living with most of my life. I saw that I had placed a wall between myself and God, and I was afraid of being fully seen by Him.

There is this beautiful painting by Del Parson that depicts Jesus Christ standing at a door, but the door has no handle.[2] It illustrates the beloved scripture "Behold, I stand at the door and knock: if any man hear my voice, and open the door, I will come in to him, and will sup with him, and he with me" (Revelations 3:20). I began to see that there was a door between The Lord and myself. And I had been the one that put it there! He had always been on the outside knocking, but it was up to me to open the door. Occasionally, I cracked open the door, but mostly I just slipped my letters underneath.

WHEN YOU HEAR THE KNOCK

Have you ever had the experience of being at home, still in your pajamas though it is long past morning, your house is a mess, you don't have makeup on, you have bed head, things feel totally chaotic, and suddenly there's a knock at your front door? How do you react? Do you confidently go to the door and open it up and invite the person inside? What is your first thought?

I have typically responded in panic! I've debated pretending I wasn't home. I've been hit with a wall of shame at the thought of being truly seen in such vulnerability, such imperfection, such a mess. I've hoped it was the UPS man already halfway back to his truck and not my perfectly-has-it-all-together neighbor dropping by for a surprise visit. I have had this same panic when I have heard the knock come from heaven. I've thought, *I can't open the door! I'm a total mess! And my house is a mess. And I need to get everything in order first. What will he think of me if He sees me like this?"*

So for many years, I carefully crafted my conversations with the door between us. Never realizing that, in His perfect love, he knocked because He desired to come in and be with me. He knocked because he desired to help clean things up and restore beauty. This wasn't a one-time visit. He intended to move right in! To live each day working together to make my world more beautiful.

I believed I couldn't fully open the door until I took care of everything on the inside first. My write-and-burn session revealed all of this to me. I suddenly began to view God in His true character. An all-knowing, all-loving, all-powerful being who loved me individually. Everything changed. The door opened wide.

None of us come into a full oneness with God without first letting go of some baggage. For me, I had to let go of my belief about how God felt about me and how I felt about myself. What you believe about these two identities—who you are and who God is—is the most important thing you can clarify in your own life. Everything hinges on this understanding.

Remember, Jesus already taught us the order to finding our identity: "love the Lord thy God with all thy heart, and with all thy soul, and with all thy strength, and with all thy mind; and [love] thy neighbour as thyself" (Luke 10:27). All other things he taught rest upon this foundation. But I was living this concept backward! I believed that if I did everything else in life right first, then I would feel love for myself, then I would feel His love for me. This doesn't work. Life only works in one direction. Love comes first. And it first comes from God. "We love him, because he first loved us" (1 John 4:19).

We were not created to be perfect on our own. Removing the door between God and ourselves is the key to everything. It's the key to mending our relationships, reaching our goals, solving problems, finding truth, healing, finding peace, making the right choices, being patient, having vision, and creating a wonderful life. It's the key, because this is where the power is. The power comes in unity. The power comes from the love of God in total eclipse of your own divinity. The power is His power in you. You are one. Have you experienced this power? The prophet Alma asks a similar question, saying, "If ye have felt to sing the song of redeeming love, I would ask, can ye feel so now?" (Alma 5:26).

Sometimes, this complete alignment can feel as rare and fleeting as a total solar eclipse. With joyful conviction, I can say that I have felt this power, and at the same time, I confess to not sustaining this alignment perfectly long term. I take comfort in the Lord comparing our glory to that of the stars and the moon. We are nothing without the Sun; we wax and we wane.

It is by design that the universe is governed upon the same principles that guide our own progression. The planets operate in perfect obedience. We, however, do not. We don't always use our agency for our highest good. We don't always live in our true identity. It is then our responsibility to master the art of getting back on course and to learn to orbit back again to face the Son. At times it may seem that this distance is too far to travel. Fortunately, God has made it possible for us to travel at the speed of light.

Journal Questions

1. Where are you currently on this spectrum of connection to God (as depicted in the pyramid graphic)?
2. Have you experienced other parts of the spectrum?

Notes

1. Annie Dillard, "Total Eclipse," *The Best American Essays of the Century*, ed. Joyce Carol Oates and Robert Atwan, (2000): 479.
2. Del Person, *Jesus at the Door* (*Jesus Knocking at the Door*), 2002, painting.

Chapter 11

Forgiveness: The Speed of Light

God forgives you the instant that you ask for it. . . . You are the one that is slow to forgive yourself." I had just finished a long day at a motivational workshop, and this offhand comment by the presenter startled me into awareness. I knew a great truth had just been spoken. His words wouldn't leave me. I pondered on them continually. I had never before considered how fast God is to forgive. Forgiveness had often felt hard and slow for me. Now I could see that the delay and discomfort I had experienced in the past were not from God holding me in my suffering but from my own slowness to receive His forgiveness and to forgive myself.

As I began to study scripture, there was evidence again and again that not only does God forgive but also he's quick to forgive. Not only does he give us grace but also he's quick to give it. Nestled into the many stories of miracles in the New Testament, Jesus responds with immediacy when the blind Bartimaeus came unto the Lord and hoped to be healed. "And Jesus answered and said unto him, What wilt thou that I should do unto thee? The blind man said unto him, Lord, that I might receive my sight. And Jesus said unto him, Go thy way; thy faith hath made thee whole. And immediately he received his sight, and followed Jesus in the way" (Mark 10:51–52).

When a leper comes to Jesus, He responds with quickness again: "And, behold, there came a leper and worshipped him, saying, Lord, if thou wilt, thou canst make me clean. And Jesus put forth his hand, and touched him, saying, I will; be thou clean. And immediately his leprosy was cleansed" (Matthew 8:2–3).

Then there was a woman who had suffered with an issue of blood for twelve years, no physician able to help her. When she saw Jesus in a crowd she "came behind him, and touched the border of his garment: and immediately her issue of blood stanched. And Jesus said, Who touched me? . . . And when the woman saw that she was not hid . . . she declared unto him before all the people for what cause she had touched him, and how she was healed immediately" (Luke 8:44–45, 47).

A lame man sat at the pool of Bethesda, a pool of water known for its healing powers. He had suffered for thirty-eight years with an infirmity and longed to be healed. He waited at the water's edge but was unable to enter the pool before another impotent person would press ahead before him. "When Jesus saw him lie, and knew that he had been now a long time in that case, he saith unto him, Wilt thou be made whole? Jesus saith unto him, Rise, take up thy bed, and walk. And immediately the man was made whole, and took up his bed, and walked" (John 5:6, 8–9).

And then there is story of Jesus walking on the water. In the dark hours just before dawn, his disciples are gathered in a ship, currently distressed from the tossing waves and wind upon the sea, when they look out upon the water to see Jesus walking toward them. "And Peter answered him and said, Lord . . . bid me come unto thee on the water. And he said, Come. And when Peter was come down out of the ship, he walked on the water, to go to Jesus. But when he saw the wind boisterous, he was afraid; and beginning to sink, he cried, saying, Lord, save me. And immediately Jesus stretched forth his hand, and caught him" (Matthew 14:28–31).

I have often pondered on the immediacy of Jesus saving Peter from sinking into the sea. The speed at which any of us sink through water is instantaneous. For Jesus to save him before he completely submerges requires, first, a knowledge beforehand of what was about to occur and, second, a speed of rescue that is beyond the speed of man. Jesus has both. He knows our own moments of sinking before they occur, and he is able to save at the speed of light.

The crowning illustration of the immediacy of God's forgiveness comes in his final moments upon the cross. Even in his own hour of greatest pain and suffering, Jesus references the very soldiers who crucify him, praying, "Father, forgive them; for they know not what they do" (Luke 23:34). The soldiers are still in the very act of murder, unrepentant and parting His raiment and casting lots, and yet His forgiveness is so immediate that it has already occurred long before they even ask. Truly, the Lord does forgive immediately.

Alma 34:31 reads, "If ye will repent and harden not your hearts, immediately shall the great plan of redemption be brought about unto you." Alma teaches us how we can receive the Lord's forgiveness and grace immediately. We must repent and harden not our hearts. We must be open to receiving. If we don't experience this immediacy, it is not due to a slow-responding God—He is immediate. It is our own hardness of heart that blocks us.

I liken God's speed of forgiveness to the speed of light. Scientifically, the speed of light is 186,282 miles per second (299,792 kilometers per second). If you could travel at the speed of light, you could go around the earth 7.5 times in one second. In theory, nothing can travel faster than light. Jesus consistently taught that He was the Light of the World. "I am the light of the world: he that followeth me shall not walk in darkness, but shall have the light of life" (John 8:12). God forgives with the speed of light! He is so beautifully quick to respond and to give. He is the light, and His light is also in you.

How quick are you to receive forgiveness for yourself? God forgives the instant that we ask. We, however, can be much slower to receive. My own pattern in the past has been to embark on my own period of suffering. I have countless times wallowed in my guilt and wrongly thought that if I inflicted a designated period of personal suffering, this would somehow make me more worthy of forgiveness because I could say to God that I had truly suffered for my choices.

I am learning to understand the fallacy of this kind of thinking. My goal should not be to extend my suffering, rather, it should be to quickly get rid of the darkness I feel. The only way to get rid of darkness is to receive light. I choose how fast I will give and receive light in my life. This principle of the speed of light can be integrated in many ways. We can, and must, be quick to receive light to live in our true identity.

I read an article a few years ago that cited a study done on the effectiveness of parenting. The number-one parenting trait that influenced children the most was parents who would admit when they had made mistakes. This concept was so fascinating to me that I began to implement it immediately. Whenever I make a wrong move in parenting—which most often comes from my impatience or raising my voice—I try to immediately state my mistake and ask for forgiveness. I confess, there are times that I am faster at this than others. Regardless, immediately seeking forgiveness has made a remarkable difference in our family.

Not too long after I began practicing this, I had an altercation with my son, who was six years old at the time. He became upset about losing a privilege and reacted by throwing a fit, screaming, and slamming doors. I myself was upset by his reaction and retreated to my bedroom to cool down. To my great surprise, a few moments later he humbly came into my room, climbed into my lap and said, "Mom, I'm sorry for yelling. I made a bad choice. Will you please forgive me?" We both cried together and simultaneously rejoiced at the renewed connection in our relationship. I was most overcome by his behavior because I knew he was modeling what he had seen me do over and over again. He had been taught to confess his mistakes and quickly seek forgiveness. We all make mistakes, we all make bad choices, and we all have things that we're working on. I invite you to consider how choosing to be fast at both giving and receiving the speed of light can bless your life.

THE ART OF GIVING AND RECEIVING

The speed of light works both directions. We must learn to be quick to receive forgiveness and quick to give forgiveness. Like any attribute or skill, this takes practice and it must be developed. One of the best places to start is increasing the speed you receive light for yourself. The more light and grace you have inside you, the more you can give to others. It starts with your ability to receive it first for yourself.

In his book *The Untethered Soul*, Michael Singer urges this same immediacy when we find ourselves offended by another. He says, "let go right then because it will be harder later. It won't be easier if you explore it or play with it, hoping to take the edge off. It won't be easier to think about it, talk about it, or try to release only part of it at a time. If you want to be free to the core of your being, you must let go right away because it will not be easier later."[1]

How fast are you at receiving forgiveness? How fast do you forgive you Do you have a pattern like I did of dragging guilt and shame around to extend suffering? When you understand identity, you know that this is no longer necessary. Prolonging forgiveness is only prolonging the experience of living in your false identity. That's all it does. There is nothing noble about it, nothing worthwhile. Extending suffering is keeping up the blocks in your heart that prevent you from receiving. Open up! Let the light in!

Do you have moments you berate yourself for something you thought, said, or did? Let it go quickly. At first, this may feel like you're letting yourself off the hook too easily. The false identity teaches you to stay in your suffering as a sign of penitence or punishment. This is unnecessary and blocks your heart. I love the LDS Bible Dictionary definition of "Repentance." It states that repentance is "a change of mind, a fresh view about God, about oneself, and about the world."[2] To truly repent is to have a fresh view about oneself. You cannot do this without letting go of the old view. Receive the speed of light immediately. Forgiveness can be fast. It can be instant. The faster you let things go, the sooner you are back to your true identity. This is what you really want: freedom, light, and truth. Be fast, as fast as the speed of light.

Empowerment Tool #10: Fast Forgiveness: The Speed of Light

God grants you instant forgiveness. Practice receiving instant forgiveness for yourself this week. Prolonging forgiveness of self or others is in effect holding the false identity in place. The moment you give and receive forgiveness, you acknowledge your true identity within.

Notes

1. Michael A. Singer, *The Untethered Soul: The Journey Beyond Yourself* (Oakland: New Harbinger Publications, 2007), 74–75.
2. *Bible Dictionary*, s.v., "repentance."

Chapter 12

The True Nature of God

Do you know why God is so fast to forgive you? He's fast because He knows who you really are. He intimately knows your true identity. He sees right through the façade of the false identity, disregarding all your mistakes and weaknesses. None of this is the real you. He only sees the truth.

Likewise, the reason we don't always quickly connect to God is that we create a false image of Him. We have spent the majority of this book learning the difference between what is true and what is false within ourselves. If being one with God is the highest level of identity, it is important that we know the truth of who God really is.

THE FALSE IMAGE OF GOD

Just as Satan entices you to create a false identity, he works tirelessly to create a false image of God. What does this look like? The false image of God includes a characterization of a being who expects flawless perfection; is disappointed in your weaknesses; disapproves of you; teaches through pain, suffering, and punishment; is far away; is critical; is always finding fault; condemns; believes you are never good enough for Him; and withholds forgiveness and love until you comply perfectly with his expectations. All of these beliefs are closed and create separation between you and God. They are counter to His true nature.

Have you ever felt the false image of God? Have you ever believed that He was far away, angry, critical of you, condemning you, punishing you, or frustrated at your lack of perfection? This is a false image of who God really is. When you are in your false identity, it's much easier to believe that God must be this way.

Just as your true identity is a place of love, joy, peace, and openness, the true character of God embodies these attributes in a fully developed form. God is the Father of your spirit; He created your true identity in His true image. In the biblical account of the creation, He says, "let us make man [and woman] in our image" (Genesis 1:26). This is true on every level. We look like our Heavenly Parents physically, and our spirits and intellects are encoded with the same power for good. The purpose of our life on earth is to develop our souls to become like our Heavenly Parents.

LIFE IS A CLASSROOM, NOT A TEST[1]

One of the great struggles of religious thought is the belief that mortal life is a pass-fail test that determines whether we are good enough to go to heaven. Our modern-day understanding of the word "test" conjures memories of how we have personally experienced being good enough or not good enough.

If you have ever auditioned, interviewed, applied for a position, or simply taken a test in school that determines your advancement, you know the feeling. You are either good enough to move forward or you're not. To have the belief that the purpose of life is this same kind of test is a misunderstanding created by the false identity. It creates immense anxiety, fear, and lack in your own life.

This life is a test, but not the kind you are familiar with. If so, every one of us has already failed. We all make mistakes, we all have weakness, and none of us has the ability to perfect ourselves by our efforts alone. God already anticipated this from the very beginning and provided a solution: a Savior. Jesus Christ turned the purpose of life from a test into a classroom.

To be specific, there is no scripture that uses the word "test." We add it into our commentary and modern translations of the Bible, but the original manuscripts do not use this word. Instead we find the word "prove." When speaking to Abraham regarding all the spirits in heaven whom He will send to earth, God says, "we will prove them herewith, to see if they will do all things whatsoever the Lord their God shall command them" (Abraham 3:25).

Today, we use the word "prove" similarly to the way we use the word "test," yet this word anciently meant something very different. The Merriam-Webster Dictionary provides an archaic definition, which gives greater understanding: "to learn or find out by experience."[2] Let's read that scripture again with the intended definition. "We will prove them herewith [in other words, we will let them learn by experience] to see if they will do all things whatsoever the Lord their God shall command them." In essence, we are here on earth to learn by experience how to listen to God and choose good over evil. Learning by experience gives lots of room for mistakes and weakness. If life were just a test, we would be doomed from the start.

Life is a classroom, not a test. The Lord is not wearing a white lab coat, observing your every action behind a glass window to see if your performance is good enough for Him. More accurately, He is the teacher in a very hands-on classroom, where the students are all having unique experiences to learn how to be like Him and to believe Him. You can approach Him at any time to receive His help, guidance, support, and encouragement. He's on your team.

If you've been worried about whether you'll make it or whether you're good enough, relax. Let go of the limiting belief that your worth is yet to be determined. Jesus Christ already established your worth when He died for you. You don't have to worry whether you'll make it. You don't have to worry whether you're good enough. You are!

Your true identity is the seed of everything God wants you to be. He planted you here to gain the experience you need to grow. This anxiety and worry come from a distant relationship with God. The closer you draw to Him, the more you are tutored in your mistakes, not condemned and left anxiously fretting on your eternal future. Instead of creating anxiety over whether the seed of who you are is good enough to pass the test, plant the seed. Put yourself in the ground. Be willing to make mistakes and learn from them. Counsel with your teacher as you gain mastery through trial and error.

As I sit with my son each afternoon for a piano lesson, it would be foolish of me to expect him to show up and play everything perfectly each day. It would be poor teaching for me to condemn him every time he made a mistake and shout at him for not knowing how to play a piece he had not yet learned or practiced long enough. This would break his spirit and discourage him from even wanting to try. It would distance our relationship, and he would never progress. I expect him to make several mistakes. I expect him to start at level one and gradually, through practice, progress to the next level. I expect him to ask questions, to come to me when he can't figure out how to play a passage. I expect to repeat phrases together over and over again until we master it together. I expect that it will take many years to reach a high level of proficiency. I expect that there will be days he will feel discouraged and want to give up. The only thing I ask is that he show up and be willing to try. Every day. We will do this together. I desire for him to gain experience and learn how to become an instrument himself.

Likewise, God is the master teacher. He does not teach through punishment and condemnation. He teaches through love and clear instruction. He forgives at the speed of light and only asks that you show up. Come unto Him and be willing to gain experience and to be guided. As soon as we stop worrying about the false identity and whether we appear good enough—to others or to God—we can actually start making some progress. When you live in your true identity and see God in His true image, growth happens. Life becomes easy. You begin to grow rapidly. Why? Because you've removed the resistance. Your false identity coupled with the false image of God are in opposition to truth. As such, this is the home of struggle and suffering. Remove it, and you are free.

THE TRUE NATURE OF GOD

The Bible Dictionary states, "The Lord has revealed Himself and His perfect character, possessing in their fulness all the attributes of love, knowledge, justice, mercy, unchangeableness, power, and every other needful thing, so as to enable the mind of man to place confidence in Him without reservation" (Bible Dictionary, "Faith"). Can you imagine placing confidence in God without reservation? This is only possible when you know His true character. When you understand God's attributes, He becomes approachable, and you can trust Him and have faith in Him.

Because the adversary continually entices us to create a false image of God, the Lord reminds us repeatedly through scripture who He really is. Let's review some of the foundational attributes of His character. God is the creator. God is merciful.

God is unchanging. God is truth. God is no respecter of persons. God is love. Now, let's break these down.

- **God Is the Creator:** God is the creator of the universe, and He is the creator of you. Because He is the greatest of all, you can put your trust in Him and have faith in His power over all things (see Genesis 1; Psalm 90:2).
- **God Is Merciful:** You may be painfully aware of your own weaknesses and mistakes. When you understand that God is merciful, you know you can come to Him in your underdeveloped state and be accepted, forgiven, and nurtured (see Psalm 103:17; Psalm 103:6–8; Exodus 34:6).
- **God Is Unchanging:** God's unchangeable nature allows you to have faith in Him because He is the same yesterday, today, and forever. Can you imagine the confusion and uncertainty of a God who did change? You would never know when His love would turn to hatred or when His commandments might change to something new. This unchangeable nature of God provides a steadiness and reliability that can always be trusted (see Malachi 3:6; James 1:17; Hebrews 1:10–12).
- **God Is Truth:** Knowing God is truth and that He cannot lie allows you to have faith and trust in His word and in His promises (see Numbers 23:19).
- **God Is No Respecter of Persons:** What does that even mean? It means that God doesn't play favorites. He loves all His children equally, regardless of behavior, race, gender, color, or any other discrimination. If God did play favorites, you would never know what your own privileges were. You would never know how far His blessings would extend to you. You would never know which commandments applied to you and which ones didn't. Because He extends His blessings and promises to all His children—you can trust that you belong and have the potential He promises you (see Acts 10:34; 2 Peter 3:9; 1 Timothy 2:4).
- **God Is Love:** Because He loves you, He is for you! He is on your team and ready to help you in all things. This attribute of love influences all His other attributes and is His reigning motivation. God told Moses, "my work and my glory [is] to bring to pass the immortality and eternal life of man" (Moses 1:39). God loves this classroom and the opportunity you have to learn through experience how to become like Him. It is His work and His glory. Can you see how the true nature of God makes Him the absolute greatest teacher? We have nothing to fear! He loves helping us and teaching us. He created this earthly experience not as a test of our worth but rather as an amazing opportunity to become who He created you to become (see 1 John 4:8).

God's true character is a far cry from the false image Satan can create in our minds. Elder Dieter F. Uchtdorf illustrated the contrast of the false and true nature of God in these words: "Part of our challenge is, I think, that we imagine that God has all of His blessings locked in a huge cloud up in heaven, refusing to give them to us unless we comply with some strict, paternalistic requirements He has set up. But the commandments aren't like that at all. In reality, Heavenly Father is constantly raining blessings upon us. It is our fear, doubt, and sin that, like an umbrella, block these blessings from reaching us."[3]

Have you ever felt this way? Certain that your lack of a particular blessing came from God refusing to shine upon you? This does not align with His true character. God is no respecter of persons. Elder Uchtdorf reveals what is truly in the way, saying it is "our fear, doubt, and sin" that block us. Fear, doubt and sin. I cannot think of a more apt description of the false identity. If fear, doubt, and sin block you, then the opposite will open you to receive. What is the opposite of fear? Faith. What is the opposite of doubt? Hope. What is the opposite of sin? Righteousness. Faith. Hope. Righteousness. I cannot think of a more apt description of your true identity.

God is constantly raining blessings upon you. Just as the sun shines upon us all—regardless of belief or behavior—His blessings are the same. He is no respecter of persons. All blessings are raining down upon you and me. Do you receive them? Or are you using an umbrella? The purpose of this book is to help you take down the umbrella. To provide the tools to clear the fears and doubts you have about yourself so your actions and results will lead you in a life of joy and peace, receiving all the blessings God is already raining upon you. Put down the umbrella and receive.

Journal Questions

1. What has been your image of God?
2. In what ways has your image of God been false? Which true attribute(s) correct that false image?
3. What influences in your life create a false image of His character?
4. What influences in your life create a true image of His character?
5. How can you increase those influences to maintain a pure image of who He is?
6. How does knowing the true character and attributes of God influence how you see yourself?

Notes

1. Kim Giles, "Lifes Test Was Turned Into a Classroom," KSL.com, December 21, 2015, https://www.ksl.com/?sid=37842526.
2. *Merriam-Webster's Collegiate Dictionary*, s.v. "prove (v.)," accessed April 28, 2018, http://www.merriam-webster.com/dictionary/prove.
3. Dieter F. Uchtdorf, "Living the Gospel Joyful," *Ensign*, Nov. 2014.

Chapter 13

Belonging

I had already been away from home for a year and half. Now, I wondered if I would ever see home again. My mission had just ended, and my parents and siblings were eager to see this beautiful part of the country. To celebrate my return, they flew out to tour the Maritime Provinces of Canada and to escort me the rest of the way home.

On our return flight to Utah, we stopped for a brief layover in Ottowa, Ontario. As we gathered around the baggage claim waiting for our bags to circulate toward us, the entire airport suddenly dulled to a stop. The bags no longer moved, the lights went out, and there was a moment of silence before the panic set in.

Little did we know that millions of other people had just experienced a similar loss of power. The Northeast blackout of 2003 affected much of the Northeast coast of the United States and Canada. At the time, it was the second largest blackout in history, causing one hundred fatalities and millions of people to be stranded without power and basic needs for more than forty-eight hours. It was not a good day for travel.

Here we were, a family of five completely stranded in a foreign country. Since this was the middle stop of our itinerary, we were now far away from the familiarity of my mission area, and I knew no one to turn to for help. All flights were grounded indefinitely, unable to function without power and ground communication. Travelers all around us spoke in alarmed tones. All of us felt disconnected and we yearned for home.

My dad gathered what information he could from airport staff and then gathered us into a huddle. We circled our luggage and counseled together on what to do. One fellow traveler had suggested renting a car and driving to Montreal, Quebec. Quebec operated from their own power grid and would have a functioning airport. We prayed together about this decision and all agreed it was the best option.

My dad left briefly to the row of car rental businesses only to find every rental closing down, having rented every last car on the lot. One business remained, and the man handed my dad the keys to their last vehicle, a van. Exactly the right size for a family of five with loads of luggage—a true tender mercy.

We anxiously piled into the van and did our best to navigate our way to Montreal. We turned on the radio to keep updated on the state of affairs now affecting an estimated fifty-five million people. Stories came in over the speakers of runs on grocery stores, drivers abandoning their vehicles after driving as far as possible before running out of gas. Gas stations raising gas prices, not knowing when they would receive more fuel. Restaurants closing from spoiled food unable to be refrigerated or cooked. People trapped in elevators. Cell phone communication unavailable. Fires started from careless use of emergency candles. The list of chaos went on and on.

Within a few hours we arrived in Montreal, thankful the drive was within distance of a single tank of gas, and joined thousands of other stranded travelers now cleaving to the Montreal airport as their final hope. My dad waited for two hours in line for a pay phone to talk to the airlines about rerouting our tickets, only to find that my own ticket, having been booked separately by the Church, would not be able to reroute with the rest of my family's. I was not considered to be part of the same travel party, and it was estimated that I would need to wait several more days in Montreal by myself.

The shock of the news was devastating to me. Beyond the alarming misadventure of trying to return home, the thought of now being separated from my family and left in a foreign city with no sense of belonging was crushing. My family home was far away, my mission home was far away, and I was soon to be left in a French-speaking city, now over trodden with stray refugees. I felt displaced and alone.

We miraculously found an available room in a nearby hotel and spent the night in a real bed, all while I prayed to not be abandoned. My family was scheduled to depart on an afternoon flight, and my ticket still hung detached and unavailable for several more days.

The following day, I accompanied my family to the airport once again. The high energy usually found in airports was replaced with the anxious hope of weary travelers, desperate to get even miles closer to their destination. We waited in another line for several hours to talk to an exhausted flight attendant who had the overwhelming job of verifying flights one by one for an endless amount of people. I leaned over the counter, expressing my desire to join my family on the upcoming flight, and she weakly muttered, "I'll see what I can do." More than twenty minutes passed as she typed into the computer and shook her head and then tried again and again. *Please let me join my family,* I silently prayed as I hovered close by, watching her every move. She tried again and again but was continually met with restrictions.

THE NEED TO BELONG

The desire for home and belonging runs deep and is considered on par with our basic needs of survival and safety. Beyond the extreme experience of separation that I had in my grand feat coming home, the fundamental need for belonging even in the day-to-day moments is a constant pulse within us all.

In 1943, American psychologist Abraham Maslow published his observation of the fundamental human needs we each require to realize our full potential. Maslow's Hierarchy of Needs has become iconic and begins with the most basic need for human survival, starting with physiological needs, safety, and the need for love and belonging. True identity, or as Maslow refers to it, "self-actualization," includes our basic need to belong.

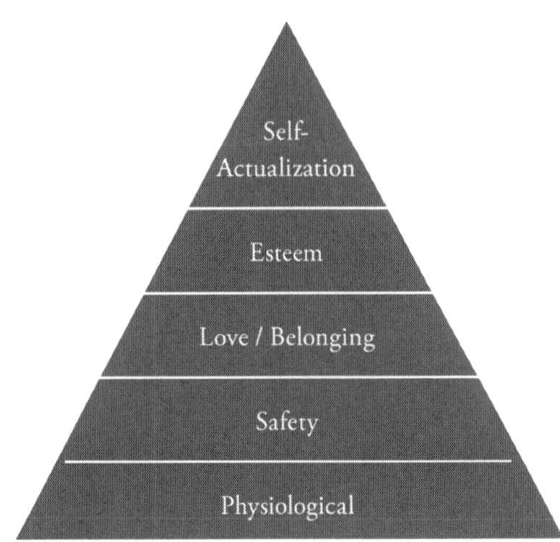

Why is this need to belong so potent? Belonging is innate and necessary for our growth and happiness. In the grand scheme of creation, we are all connected. We were all created by God. He is our Father, and we are His children. We are wired with a homing instinct that urges us to find our way back to our Heavenly Family, and thus we seek belonging. Yet the adversary tries to persuade us to find belonging in the wrong places and wrong ways. Soon enough the false identity whispers that we don't belong in the very places that have potential to help us return: our families, churches, and communities.

We must learn to channel the need for belonging in a way that truly unites and empowers. Belonging begins in our relationship to God. You must know He loves you and accepts you. From there, you can expand your circle to the rest of your brothers and sisters of the world. Unfortunately, it's common for us to switch the order, seeking belonging first from other people and then wondering why our sense of belonging lacks stability. Perhaps you have felt this fleeting sense of belonging in your own circles.

DIFFERENCES VERSUS SIMILARITIES

Years ago, I was balancing a life of young motherhood and entrepreneurship. I spent most of my time reading books, articles, and watching videos to help me learn the skills I needed to improve my work. My business was my life.

By invitation from a friend at church, I began to attend a weekly playgroup at a community park with other young moms. Conversation in the group hovered around mothering topics such as potty training, meal planning, and budgeting. While these issues are an obvious part of my day to day, I found little stimulation talking about it. I quickly realized that I was the only working mom in the bunch and isolated myself in my thoughts. I felt like I didn't belong. I couldn't relate to anyone. They couldn't relate to me. I was different. I didn't belong in this group. No one understood me. No one shared the same interest in business, and I couldn't possibly connect if I was so very different from them.

I found that emphasizing my differences created a wide divide. Like a broken piece of ice floating further and further away from the massive iceberg, each difference I dwelled upon drifted me apart from the larger whole. It wasn't until I flipped my focus 180 degrees and began to look for the ways we were the same, that connection came within reach again.

THE BODY OF CHRIST

There is a delicate dance between the need for individuality and the need for community in this quest for belonging. Like the tension between how we are the same and how we are different, it is the polarity that actually holds us together in the perfect balance.

The Apostle Paul, in writing to the Corinthians, likened this dichotomy to being a part of the Body of Christ. He describes the unique calling of each individual, saying:

> Just as a body, though one, has many parts, but all its many parts form one body, so it is with Christ.
>
> Even so the body is not made up of one part but of many.
>
> Now if the foot should say, "Because I am not a hand, I do not belong to the body," it would not for that reason stop being part of the body.
>
> And if the ear should say, "Because I am not an eye, I do not belong to the body," it would not for that reason stop being part of the body.
>
> If the whole body were an eye, where would the sense of hearing be? If the whole body were an ear, where would the sense of smell be?
>
> But in fact God has placed the parts in the body, every one of them, just as he wanted them to be.
>
> If they were all one part, where would the body be?
>
> But God has put the body together. . . .
>
> So that there should be no division in the body, but that its parts should have equal concern for each other.

> If one part suffers, every part suffers with it; if one part is honored, every part rejoices with it.
>
> Now you are the body of Christ, and each of you is a part of it. (1 Corinthians 12:12, 14–19, 24–27 NIV)

Paul beautifully illustrates the unique contribution we make as individuals to a greater whole.

We are all different and we are all one. Belonging comes when you have an understanding of your unique contribution to the greater whole and a vision for what the greater whole really is. If you never know you are part of the body, you will never understand how you contribute.

THE ECONOMY OF BELONGING: GIVE & RECEIVE

It is important for you to do the work to discover your own unique gifts. What part do you play? What fascinating qualities do you bring to the world? Are you the hand? The foot? The mouth? The eye? The ear? The smile?

"For all have not every gift given unto them; for there are many gifts, and to every man is given a gift by the Spirit of God. To some is given one, and to some is given another, that all may be profited thereby" (D&C 46: 11–12). You are intentionally unique. You are different. You have been endowed with your own gifts to serve the world. When you can see your differences in context of abundance, you understand that you bring a unique contribution to the whole. You belong in a wonderful way.

When you see your differences as lacking, you hide your gifts, begrudgingly back away, and separate yourself. You may wonder why your gifts are different from others' gits, unable to see that what is missing is you!

This distribution of unique gifts creates a currency "that all may be profited thereby." You need not possess a gift to benefit from the gift. The benefit comes in giving and receiving. It's a currency. An exchange. You are profited when you receive from another. Others profit when they receive from you.

This economy of sharing the gifts of your true identity rests upon your willingness to give and receive. This economy crashes when you allow fear and scarcity to prevent an exchange. And just as Paul prophesied, "if one part suffers, every part suffers with it; if one part is honored, every part rejoices with it."

RESONANCE

When you experience this synergy of belonging, you experience resonance. High resonance occurs when the exchange of give and receive is in unrestrained flow. You feel free to share and free to receive from one another. Have you experienced this in your dearest relationships? You feel complete freedom to be in your true identity, confide, and contribute because you know that you will be received well and profit from the other person in return. You feel safe and loved. You belong.

Low resonance comes from an imbalance in this exchange. You or the other person holds back from giving or receiving. Perhaps fear creeps in, or the false identity warns that you won't be accepted, and so you withdraw from giving or receiving. Have you experienced this in your relationships?

Resonance can be found both as a natural connection and as a cultivated one. Because we fluctuate in our ability to give and receive, the resonance of our relationships can change as well. If you desire more resonance in your relationship with your spouse, child, friend, colleague, or community, look for ways to increase the give and receive and watch the resonance of belonging increase.

We naturally resonate higher or lower among the variety of people in our world. It's a guidance system to help you navigate to the people you most need in your life. When high resonance occurs, it's a celebration and a true gift. It's how you find your people and your own circle of belonging. High resonance is a great indication for choosing who to marry, who to bring into your closest group of friends, who to trust and build a community with.

We often resonate high with people who can help us nurture our own gifts. Resonance is my guide for choosing what books to read, what topics to learn, what podcasts to listen to, who to spend time with, and which relationships are important for me to cultivate.

CULTIVATING BELONGING

But what about the times you feel like you don't belong? When resonance is low and belonging feels out of reach? I recently sat in a Relief Society meeting where the class discussed the topic of belonging. "How many of you feel like you don't belong here?" the teacher asked. A shocking display of hands rose. Hands of people who regularly came to church, hands of people whose lives seemed so put together. For the next thirty minutes, vulnerable feelings were shared among women of all ages, confessing the circumstances they felt separated them, coupled with the desire to feel more belonging in their church community. Sometimes we think we are the only one, and in a moment of trust, we learn that others feel the same. A strange feeling of connection settled upon us simply from realizing that we weren't alone in the struggle.

To cultivate belonging, you must participate in the economy through giving and receiving. This alone indicates the health of every community. There is a continuous outward and inward flow. You must give and you must receive. If you believe you can profit from every person in your circle, you become open to receiving. When you understand your own unique gifts to contribute, you become open to giving. This is the heart of belonging.

Giving of your true identity requires courage and can take many forms. You give by sharing your gifts, sharing your heart, sharing your presence. A willingness to show up as you and not your false identity is a generous act of giving. Receiving requires your own openness. Gone are the barriers of defense and protection, and you allow people into your own heart. Receiving is just as brave as giving, for it requires trust to let someone in.

This act of cultivating belonging is work. Your heart and mind must be regularly purged of the blocks that prevent you from giving and receiving. Yet again, the art of self-care and routine practice of empowerment and clearing tools are fundamental in allowing you to maintain your ability to give and receive.

Whenever I start to feel like I don't belong in any of my circles, I first look to myself. What do I believe that makes me feel this way? What story I am telling myself that makes me feel this way? How can I write a new story? Am I truly giving? Am I truly receiving?

START WITH BELONGING TO GOD

Because we're human, we struggle to maintain belonging. There are times even when the high resonance we feel with those closest to us will be less. Yet, there is one who is steady and perfect in giving and receiving. There is one to whom we always belong.

The true nature of God is love. He is constantly giving, and His arms are always outstretched to receive us. When you come to know God in His true nature and nurture your relationship to Him, you find belonging of the most enduring kind. My own sense of belonging to God has been grounded through the simple mantra, "I love and accept you, Brooke." I mentioned this mantra meditation earlier as an empowerment tool in chapter 6. I quickly discovered in my daily practice that these words are more than a pep talk of my true identity trying to convince me of my worth. These words come from someone greater than I am.

As I practice this meditation, I have transitioned to repeating these words in my mind while visualizing them coming from Jesus Christ. As soon as I imagined this mantra to come from Him, I began to develop a deeply personal connection to Him. I felt grounded in the truth of these words and I found "home." I also found a deeper connection to other people, *after* I found belonging to the Lord.

My foundation is now solid, and regardless of what happens around me, I always have a connection to home. I belong to Him. Always. He is unchanging, which means His love and acceptance of me is unchanging. This mantra is always true. Even when my false identity masquerades briefly, I still belong to Him. I practice fast forgiveness of myself and realign to truth.

As I stood at the airport counter in my dramatic journey home, prayerfully watching the compassionate flight attendant searching to reconfigure my journey, I felt a conviction for home like never before. Home wasn't a place as much as it was being part of my family. The thought of being separated from them was far more grievous than never making it back to my house in Utah. I longed for belonging. Home was where belonging was. Finally, after one last try, the flight attendant gave a sigh of relief. A tiny smile crossed her face, and she handed me a boarding pass. "I want you to go home with your family," she whispered. I started to cry. We'd be together after all.

Jesus taught again and again, "the kingdom of God is within you" (Luke 17:21). The kingdom of God is home. It is where God dwells, and it is always inside you. You are part of His family. When you awaken to your divine nature and live in your true identity, you find belonging. It was there all along. Welcome home.

Afterword

Who Builds Your Identity?

Today, my worth and identity are no longer dependent on outside validation and approval. Does this mean I no longer struggle?

During the period of writing this book, I simultaneously experienced the distraction of the false identity telling stories and whispering deception. *You're not smart enough to write a book. Everyone already knows this stuff.* I renewed my social media fast for four months (and counting!) in order to quiet the false identity enough to finish this book. It seems that stepping outside your comfort zone is a big trigger to the voice of discouragement.

Yes, I still have two wolves inside—yet having tools and knowing the truth of who I really am has allowed me to distinctly know the difference between the two. I try valiantly to daily nourish myself in self-care and empowerment tools, while also quieting my false identity through clearing tools. I work at this every day, and my identity feels the difference. While the false identity is still there, it is weaker from not being fed regularly.

One early morning during this book-writing period, I had a dream. I stood on a beautiful beach and a trusted figure appeared to me, inviting me to follow her. She motioned towards a door, seemingly hidden in the cavity of a cliff nearby. Pushing aside overgrown vines, she pulled on the rusted metal ring and the door squeaked, opening with hesitation from years of neglect as we both stepped inside.

A cave-like tunnel stretched before us, and I could see light in the distance, leading to the world on the other side. She walked ahead of me, leading the way in confident silence, eyes fixed on the light. Immediately, I became aware of thousands of little eyes staring down at me from the ceiling and sides of the tunnel, and I began to make out the details of scrawny tiny gremlins reaching out towards me with their shriveled arms as they clung to the dark, moist earth of the tunnel. Somehow, I understood that they could not hurt me or touch me unless I allowed them to. I felt their presence and shuddered onward as I focused instead upon the light ahead.

In great relief, we reached the other side, and I stepped out to see a vast expanse of a mountainous valley and a majestic city nestled in the safety of the valley floor.

I longed to go there, but my guide led me instead to a nearby bluff, covered in black ash, vacant of any vegetation or life.

There stood a ramshackle house, old and dilapidated. I reached for the door handle and opened it to step inside. Instantly, the house collapsed to the earth, each board creating a cloud of dust and debris in the sudden crash. With pieces of the house now at my feet, I could see another house next door.

I walked to the next house, also rickety and poorly built. I approached the door to step inside, but it instantly turned to sand, losing its form into piles of dust on the ground. Another house appeared next. I reached out to open the door, but the house vanished into thin air. Another house remained, but before I could even touch it, it burst into violent flames.

At this point I was feeling rather discouraged and irritable. There was a growing need inside me to find a home. I looked about and caught sight of a beautiful home in the distance. It was perched precariously atop a tall, skinny mountain. I instantly found myself inside. The views out the windows overlooked the valley and ocean in the distance. The home was built to shiny perfection, a stark contrast to the weak, old homes that self-destructed in moments. As much as I wanted to stay here, I feared moving and walking about would tip the house to its demise off the Dr.-Seuss-like precipice it was now balanced upon. With no suitable house, I retreated back to an open field and embraced the safety of solid ground and open space.

After I awoke, the vivid scenes remained clearly in my mind, coupled with a desire to discern what it could mean. As I reflected and prayed for an interpretation, awareness unveiled in my mind. I saw the adversarial gremlins that reach out to the false identity, preoccupying it and preventing it from reaching the light. I saw each house as an identity I could live within. Whether it was an identity of weakness or an identity of shiny perfection atop a pedestal, none were safe or lasting.

Moments after praying for understanding, I stumbled upon a quote from C. S. Lewis that felt like a crowning jewel of insight:

> Imagine yourself as a living house. God comes in to rebuild that house. At first, perhaps, you can understand what He is doing. He is getting the drains right and stopping the leaks in the roof and so on: you knew that those jobs needed doing and so you are not surprised. But presently he starts knocking the house about in a way that hurts abominably and does not seem to make sense. What on earth is He up to? The explanation is that He is building quite a different house from the one you thought of—throwing out a new wing here, putting on an extra floor there, running up towers, making courtyards. You thought you were going to be made into a decent little cottage: but He is building a palace. He intends to come and live in it Himself.[1]

I am reminded again and again that God can make me far better than I can make myself. How many times have I tried to build my own identity? How often have I searched for a better house? Yet when I finally let go of my own plans and allow the Lord to build me instead—trusting His vision and intention—I am awed at the resulting creation. It is more beautiful than anything I could imagine.

NOTE

1. C. S. Lewis, *Mere Christianity* (New York: HarperOne, 1980), 205, borrowed from the parable of George Macdonald.

Acknowledgments

This book is evidence to the power of vision. Thanks goes to my dear friend Kristi Drennan, who saw the vision well before I did and held it clearly for me from conception to completion.

Thanks to my friend Davina Fear for teaching me about belonging and the integral role it plays for living in your true identity.

Thanks to all my original students in my Identity 101 course. Your response to this information fueled my commitment to create this message in book form to make it accessible to more people. Your encouragement and desire to share this with others meant the world.

Thanks to Stephanie Romney, Robyn Rusch, and Emily Hanks. Your play-dates were service that gifted me time to meet deadlines and have some peace of mind.

Thanks to Esther Raty for miraculously finding me.

Thanks to my team at Cedar Fort Publishing, most especially my incredible editors, Kaitlin Barwick, Valene Wood, and Breanna Call Herbert. Your polishing touch made all the difference.

Thanks to Dr. Dean Madsen and Lynn Blake. You always saw my true identity, even when I couldn't, and it changed the course of my life.

Thanks to my parents, Don and Barbie Corbridge. You lived with my false self longer than anyone and you loved me anyway. Thank you for always pointing me to who I really was and could become.

Thanks to my writing angels.

Thanks to Jacob and Sarah. Your true identities are the light of my life.

Thanks to my steady husband, Ben. You always support my projects and big visions. My favorite vision is the life we share together as a family.

Thanks to my Heavenly Father and Jesus Christ for creating this amazing classroom of life and making it possible to truly become who You created me to become. I'm continuously amazed at just how glorious this visionary plan really is.

About the Author

Brooke Snow is a writer, speaker, podcaster, and prolific online educator, having taught more than 3,500 students in her online classes in both personal growth and photography. Brooke has a gift of seeing the big picture and extracting life lessons from each experience. She is a wife, a mother of two, and a survivor, and has triumphed over PTSD and anxiety. She believes all people can change and that we hold the power to create the life we want.

Scan to visit

blog.brookesnow.com